DYNAMICS IN PSYCHOLOGY

Dynamics in Psychology

By
WOLFGANG KÖHLER

AUTHOR OF
Gestalt Psychology,
The Place of Value in a World of Facts

LIVERIGHT
NEW YORK

ISBN: 0-87140-087-1
Library of Congress Catalog Card Number: 72-96903

Liveright Paperbound Edition 1973

1.987654321

Manufactured in the United States of America

PREFACE

THESE chapters contain a discussion of psychological theory and its function in psychological work. The way in which I interpret the relation between theory and factual research is exemplified by two instances. The first introduces Faraday's views into the theory and investigation of perception, the second applies the same concepts to problems of memory.

I feel greatly indebted to the University of Virginia for the honor of having been invited to deliver the Page-Barbour Lectures of 1938. The present chapters represent a slightly amplified version of the actual lectures.

To Professor and Mrs. M. Mandelbaum I wish to express my thanks for invaluable help in transforming my English into a readable text. Dr. Hans Wallach has been an indefatigable collaborator in the experimental work which is described in the second chapter. I am also grateful to him for the preparation of the figures which will assist the reader in following the argument of this book. My wife has done untiring work as typist.

SWARTHMORE,   WOLFGANG KÖHLER.
May 1939

DYNAMICS IN PSYCHOLOGY

THE WAYS OF PSYCHOLOGY

I

WE ALL have our moods, our ups and downs. Once during a conversation I found a colleague of mine, a psychologist, in a particularly despondent condition. "In our field," he said, "have any important discoveries been made that could compare with those of the natural sciences? An entirely new branch of physics developed, you know, when the physicists discovered what we now call electric currents. But this is just one example. During the last hundred years, startling revelations have followed each other in physics at an amazing speed. When we both were children, science discovered X-rays and radioactivity. Since then the discovery of the *quantum* has revolutionized the whole system of physics. You will not be able to point to a single new fact in psychology which has in the same manner revealed the existence of unknown territory. For some reason we are obviously incapable of achieving in our field what one generation of physicists after another has been doing as a matter of course."

I have heard similar remarks more than once. They

seem to me based on an unfortunate misunderstanding. The physical facts to which my colleague pointed will under ordinary circumstances scarcely occur in our environment. When they occur they will remain unnoticed: in the first place because as a rule their intensity is too low; in the second place because our sense organs do not directly announce their presence. These organs are little sensitive to precisely such facts. Thus these facts have to be discovered.

There are, however, other physical facts which need not be discovered by the physicists, because every normal human being becomes familiar with them by common experience. Thus we all know without the help of physics that objects fall when they are not supported; that many objects tend to move as wholes when they are struck by other objects; that under such impact certain objects tend to break; that after a temporary distortion some things will return to their original shape; that rubbing will make objects warmer, and so forth. We know about these events because they occur over and over again, because our sense organs readily announce their presence, and because in this manner they become objects of immediate and ever-repeated awareness.

When we realize that there are these two kinds of facts in physics we can easily see why the psychologists are unable to point to entirely new territories which have been discovered by their research. The reason is not that such discoveries are more difficult in psychology than they are in physics; nor should we believe that psychologists lack the skill and the initiative which discoverers need. Rather there have been no psychological discoveries in this sense simply because man was acquainted with practically all territories of mental life a long time before the founding of scientific psychology. In other words, psychologists could not make such startling discoveries as constitute the pride of physics, because at the very beginning of their work there were no entirely unknown mental facts left which they could have discovered.

Everybody is familiar with the principal human drives, with habit and memory, with moods and emotions, with thinking and attention, with sleep and with dreams. Even if not all people come in direct contact with serious cases of neurosis and psychosis, these mental disturbances could not remain generally unknown, because their symptoms are too striking and the patients too numerous. Even the hypnotic state is in some cases so easily produced that many were well acquainted with its characteristics long before psychology became a science. Under these circumstances, what wholly new facts could the psychologists discover? Why should we assume that any such facts are left? It seems quite possible that no discoveries in this sense will occur even in the future of our science.

Among those psychological phenomena with which we are familiar, not a few may deserve at least the same attention as is given in physics, say, to radio-activity and to X-rays. I should think that this holds for reasoning, and one might say that even the simplest achievements of memory are intrinsically quite as remarkable as are those astounding physical facts. We do not, however, look upon reasoning and on memory with the same interest as is aroused by those discoveries in physics. We take such mental facts for granted, just as we take it as a matter of course that objects fall when they are not supported, or that rubbing makes them warmer. In this respect practically *all* basic facts of mental life are compara-ble with the over-familiar kind of physical facts; and there seems to be nothing like radioactivity and X-rays among the mental phenomena, merely because the radioactivity and the X-rays of psychology have long since become a matter of general knowledge.

It seems to follow that psychology must be in a most enviable position because it starts on a level of broad information which natural science could only gradually attain by its discoveries of hidden facts. From this point of view, one might think, psychology should in spite of its youth as a science be about as far advanced as are physics and chemistry. Since this is not the case, there must be some particular difficul-ties which delay the progress of psychology. For our present purpose it will suffice if we discuss merely one of these retarding factors.

To a degree one can distinguish between psychological facts as such and psychological facts of functional dependence. By psychological facts as such I mean our experiences of all kinds. Now it is quite true that in many instances we *experience* the functional relationship of certain psychological facts. To this extent, I must admit, the two classes of psychological facts are not mutually exclusive. Facts of functional dependence *may* belong to the class of psychological facts as such. In countless cases, however, psychological facts as such are vividly experienced, whereas of their dependence on other facts there is no immediate awareness whatsoever. In other words, we do not generally know why our experiences are *as* they are, because they tell us little about their genesis. To use again an analogy from physics: Everybody knows that objects will fall if they are not supported. But, although they actually fall to the ground, it took mankind a long time to realize that "the ground" plays an active conditioning rôle in the event. *Falling* is a common fact, but *gravitation,* a fact of functional dependence, is not directly observed. In the same manner, many psychological facts of functional dependence are not themselves matters of immediate awareness; they may remain for long entirely hidden even though the experiences which thus depend on certain unrecognized conditions are, as such, thoroughly familiar facts.

Now, one of the main tasks which psychology has to solve consists in the discovery of those functional relations which are responsible for the occurrence and the characteristics of our experiences. We want to know not merely *what* happens in mental life but also *how* and *why* it happens. And from this point of view any number of discoveries are possible in psychology. Moreover in this respect the work of psychology seems to be at least as hard as is that of any other science. Curiously enough, one of the principal reasons for this is precisely the condition which seems at first to constitute a facilitating factor, namely, the extreme familiarity of psychological experiences as such. The reason is this: hidden facts of dependence will seldom be revealed by accident. They will be discovered when people ask questions about observed facts. And people do not tend to ask any questions about facts with which they are thoroughly acquainted; they ask questions about unusual events, about things which differ strikingly from familiar facts. Since we are, at least as adults, entirely familiar with most psychological data as such, there will be few occasions on which these experiences strike us as strange, and thus evoke a questioning attitude. This, I believe, is one of the major difficulties with which psychology has been confronted up to the present time. More than 2000 years ago Greek philosophers recognized that to wonder, to be startled, is the primary condition that leads to inquiry. In a realm where hardly any occurrence is ever *quite* new, few questions about the genesis of things are likely to be asked. From this point of view it would actually favor the advance of our science if some of its material were at first hidden, were then discovered, and could thus cause one astonished question after another. Here is one example that does not belong to psychology proper but illustrates the same principle: When did the reader first ask himself why the letters are arranged in the alphabet in just the sequence which we all know? I will confess that I was about 40 years old when I first heard the question mentioned, and that I do not know whether it would ever have occurred to me spontaneously. We learn the alphabetic sequence in early childhood, and when we are adults the very familiarity of this sequence prevents us from recognizing the problem which it offers. Incidentally, apart from minor variations our alphabet is an extremely old possession of western civilization. Thus this question is as interesting in the history of culture as are the hidden facts of dependence in psychology.

I shall now discuss a few instances in which psychologists have been able to reveal hidden facts of dependence, and some others in which the need of similar discoveries will be easily realized. In choosing these instances I was little influenced by a consideration of what cases would appear particularly essential from a general human point of view. I had to select examples which clearly demonstrate certain principles, which at the same time allow of comparatively simple presentation, and which are not now objects of unsettled disputes among the psychologists. It is this third point which excluded some of the more important advances that psychology has made in recent years.

II

Among the perceptual facts with which we are thoroughly familiar is the movement of objects in the visual field. Visual movement, as we perceive it daily, does not seem to deserve any particular interest. A physical object changes its place, and as its image glides over the retina of our eye we perceive a visual motion that is to all appearances directly correlated with this displacement of the retinal image. Psychologists, however, are no longer able to hold this view. I shall not try to describe all the particular facts by which our confidence in the simple commonplace nature of visual movement has been destroyed. It seems preferable to concentrate on one discovery which demonstrates with convincing clearness that the apparent obviousness of visual movement is entirely deceptive.

This discovery was made by J. F. Brown.[1] In a recent paper D. Cartwright has given the following account of Brown's observations which I shall slightly abbreviate and adapt for the present purpose.

"In a dark screen a rectangular opening was cut, immediately behind which a white paper moved

[1] J. F. Brown, Psychol. Forsch. *10* (1927); *14* (1931).

evenly and parallel to the longer of the edges of the opening. On the paper, black circles—or other figures —were fastened in a row, as a rule at equal distances from each other. The observer was asked to compare the speed of these objects with the speed of a second row of objects which moved through the opening of another screen.... (This) second opening with the pattern which was seen through it represented a replica of the first opening and its content in changed dimensions. Both screens were at the same distance from the observer." The experiments were made in a darkened room in which little besides the white openings and the patterns within them was visible. "When the two movements...were shown in different directions of space, so that comparison was successive..., a striking difference of speed appeared," even though the physical velocities were equal. "The movement of the larger circles in the larger opening was now much slower than that of the smaller circles in the smaller rectangle." This difference could be measured by varying one of the two physical velocities until both movements had visually the same speed. "When changing linear dimensions at the ratios

$$1 : 2 : 3 : 4 : 5 : 10$$

Brown had to give the objective velocities in the larger fields the relative values

$$1.9 \quad 2.6 \quad 3.1 \quad 3.5 \quad 6.8.$$

These figures represent averages for a group of subjects." [1] They prove that widely different physical velocities give rise under these circumstances to the same visual speed. It follows on the other hand that, if a certain physical velocity is given, the corresponding visual speed will vary in about the same proportions, depending upon the nature of the surrounding frame and on that of the moving objects. In a movement-field that is linearly 10 times as great as another movement-field the same physical movement will, according to these results, appear to have merely about one seventh of the speed which it has in the other, the smaller, field. The displacements of the retinal images during movement are in such experiments approximately proportional to the physical velocities of the objects themselves. We see, therefore, that between visual speed and the velocity of retinal displacements there is by no means that simple relation which most people are likely to take for granted.

Our everyday familiarity with visual movement as such is of course wholly compatible with the fact that ordinarily we have not the slightest suspicion of such secrets in the nature of visual speed. Under the conditions of common life we see movements with certain speeds, but we do not experience that these speeds depend on more or less remote circumstances. In a given and constant environment the visual speed of an object will vary in approximate proportion to

[1] D. Cartwright, Psychol. Forsch. 22 (1938), pp. 320 f.

the physical velocity. We become aware of the actual influence which the environment has on the speed of the object only if we compare in various environments visual speeds that correspond to measured physical velocities. And who has any incentive to do such a thing in the case of perceptual facts which *appear* to be quite simple, "normal," and in a way "self-contained," i.e., independent of any conditions beyond their own locus? Thus in everyday life there is for the most part nothing that could reveal the functional relationship which has been discovered by Brown. Moreover Brown found that if two movements of the same physical velocity are *simultaneously* seen, they tend to assume the *same* visual speed, even though their immediate environments are quite different. This fact makes it even less likely that we spontaneously discover the influences which surrounding objects exert on the visual speed of a given movement. No wonder, therefore, that Brown himself first made his discovery by accident, in the sense that at the time his subjects were comparing visual speeds for another reason.

A most plausible interpretation of this "Brown-effect" has been given by K. Koffka.[1] From certain observations K. Duncker had concluded that it is not the displacement of an image on the retina which as such makes us see an object as moving. Rather the

[1] K. Koffka, *Principles of Gestalt Psychology* (1935), pp. 288-291, particularly 290.

decisive factor is a change of distance between two or more objects.[1] This may lead to a visual movement of those objects whose retinal images are actually displaced; but it may also make those objects appear as moving whose retinal images are stationary. Under the conditions of Brown's experiments the screens with their openings remain stationary in the visual field, and the patterns which actually move are also seen as moving. It seemed to Koffka that Duncker's principle could be applied in the following manner to Brown's experimental situation: When an object moves through an opening its distance from the contours of this opening will on the average be greater the larger the field or opening is. We know, however, that human sensitivity to changes of distance is, roughly speaking, inversely proportional to the size of the distances which are being changed. A given small change in the length of a line will be more easily seen if this line is short than is the case if this line is much longer.[2] Since it is probable that the same holds for mere empty distances it will follow that human vision is more sensitive to changes of distances in a small field than it is to those in a large one. Changes of distance, however, are according to Duncker the causes of visual movement. Consequently a given small displacement of an object will constitute a more effective movement-stimulus in

[1] K. Duncker, Psychol. Forsch. *12*, p. 180 f. (1929).
[2] This means that to some extent Weber's law holds for the just noticeable changes of a length or a distance.

Brown's narrower fields than it does in larger openings. In other words, if we wish to give an object a certain visual speed within a large field we shall have to move it through a greater stretch per unit of time than will be needed in the case of a smaller field; i.e., within the large field we shall have to move it objectively faster. This is precisely the relationship which Brown actually discovered.

This explanation has recently been corroborated by D. Cartwright.[1] If the explanation is correct our sensitivity to changes of position of an object must depend upon the size of the field within which the object is located. And this must hold just as much for our judgment about stationary objects as, according to the explanation, it holds in the case of movement. More particularly our sensitivity to changes of position, or the accuracy with which we recognize a given position, should in fields of different sizes be proportional to the visual speed to which a given physical movement gives rise in the same fields. Brown found, for instance, that, if the sizes of two fields are linearly in the ratio 1 : 3, the visual speed in the smaller field is on the average 2.6 times as great as that in the larger opening, when physical velocity is the same in both. Cartwright reports that the accuracy with which his subjects determined the center of an opening with the (relative) linear size 1 was on the average 2.7 times as great as that with

[1] D. Cartwright, *loc. cit.*

which the same task was solved in an opening of the linear size 3. The sensitivity for changes of position therefore seems to vary in fields of different sizes precisely as does visual speed. Thus Koffka's explanation appears as adequate.[1]

What can we learn from this example? The most obvious lesson is that in spite of our familiarity with visual speed as such we are as a rule not aware of important factors on which visual speed actually depends. This dependence is not directly given when the visual speed as such is given. It can be revealed merely by indirect experimental procedures. And in this sense psychology is just as able to discover entirely unknown facts as is physics or any other science. Psychologists cannot and need not discover visual speed; everybody is familiar with it. But they can and must discover facts of functional relationship with which nobody becomes spontaneously acquainted. In the present case the discovery of such a relationship gives a well-known experience an entirely new appearance. Visual speed, which seems to be an altogether banal datum, is shown to depend on a wide context. Our next examples will prove that this is by no means an exceptional case. A great many familiar psychological facts will not be functionally understood until in their case, too, we discover con-

[1] Brown himself has given a different interpretation of his discovery. Cf. Psychol. Forsch. *14* (1931), pp. 233 ff.

nections and dependences to which ordinary experience has no access.

III

Here is another apparently trivial fact: If a letter, a book, or a newspaper, a photograph or another picture happens to come into our hands upside down we immediately turn it around. On being asked why we do so we should probably be astonished and should say: "Why, it was upside down, was it not? So it had to be turned." We are thoroughly familiar with this situation, and we know how to deal with it. But does this lead to any questions in our minds? Not in the least. The very familiarity of the situation makes it difficult for us to realize that it contains a problem.

And yet there is a problem. The shape of figures, whether they are objects in a picture or words on a page, is objectively defined by the spatial, and perhaps some other, relationships which exist among all their parts.[1] When these relationships are given, the structure of the shape is thereby determined. In what respect is this structure objectively changed if we turn it upside down? Obviously it is not changed at all. We have therefore every reason to ask ourselves why it makes a great difference in perception whether we are shown figures upside down or in what we call

[1] I should perhaps add in passing that certain "relations of relations" will have to be indicated if the objective definition of a shape is to be quite adequate for psychological purposes.

their normal orientation. In the first case we turn the objects around, because otherwise their recognition would be difficult. But as yet we do not see why it should be more difficult in the first case than it is in the second.

Our interest will, however, be intensified by a further observation. In their earliest years children do not as a rule turn pictures around which they happen to hold upside down. They seem to enjoy them about as much in this orientation as in the position which the adult would single out as normal. Parents and nurses must have seen this many times. But it was not until 1909 that the significance of this particular behavior of children was clearly recognized. The late Professor W. Stern then pointed out that children at the age of about 1½ to 4 years actually recognize objects in an "abnormal" position much more easily than do adults.[1] In this sense they are for once capable of higher achievements than we are.

As an explanation of this difference between children and adults I have often heard it said that the visual space of an individual must have a history. Originally, this argument proceeds, visual space is probably as homogeneous as is astronomical space in Newton's theory. Just as in astronomy the terms above and below, right and left, have no sensible application, the visual space of children has at first no upper and lower side, no right as qualitatively

[1] W. Stern, Zeitschr. f. angew. Psychol. 2 (1909), p. 498ff.

distinguished from a left side. If, therefore, the image of an object is turned on the retina no change whatsoever occurs in the homogeneous medium which visual space represents in a baby; as a percept the object remains for him exactly what it was before. Later in life, on the other hand, visual space acquires characteristics which are due to extravisual experiences, so that it is no longer merely visual space. Our movements, and consequently also our kinesthetic experiences, occur under the constant, directed, and one-sided influence of gravitation. Besides, movements on or toward the left side are characteristically different from movements on or toward the right side. Motor space has in this sense an inhomogeneous structure; it has its above and below, its downward and its upward direction, its right and its left. By some form of learning this ever-present structure of motor space will be transferred to visual space, until the visual field, too, becomes inhomogeneous, and its contents acquire a lower and an upper, a left and a right side. Figures now no longer remain the same when their images are turned around on the retina because under these circumstances their various parts change their relations with regard to those acquired characteristics of visual space.

If this is true we have before us one more case in which the actual constitution of perceptual facts is not revealed by their appearance as such. Visual space *itself* seems to have its lower and its upper side;

the appearance of visual objects *as such* seems to change when they are turned upside down. In this sense perceptual experience again does not point to any wider functional context, within which visual space acquires such characteristics and visual objects become dependent on orientation. And yet it seems obvious that such a wider context exists.

But we have to go further. The explanation which I have just mentioned is not wholly satisfactory. In the first place I find it hard to believe that at the age of 3 or 4 years children should still have much to learn about that structure of space to which we allude when we use the terms above and below. Apart from just those observations with which we are here concerned, their behavior shows no evidence of any uncertainty in this respect. As a matter of fact we have an amusing proof of children's acquaintance with the directed structure of space:

Gellermann [1] trained two children, who were no more than 2 years old, and two chimpanzees, who were considerably older, to choose between an equilateral triangle and another figure. These figures were shown in a vertical plane, and the triangle, the "positive" figure which the subjects learned to choose, rested on its base. When learning had been completed the experimenter introduced a change of conditions: before the next experiment the triangle was turned by 60°—or 180°, which in the case of this particular figure leads to the same result. In the new situation all subjects, the chimpanzees and the children, showed the same reaction. When looking

[1] L. W. Gellermann, Journ. of Genet. Psychol. *42* (1933).

THE WAYS OF PSYCHOLOGY

at the triangle they turned, after a moment of hesitation, their heads about 60° so as to re-establish the familiar relation between the figure and their heads. This proves not only that they recognized the triangle—they would not turn their heads in the case of an arbitrarily chosen unknown figure—it also proves that they were accurately aware of its changed orientation in space.[1] Obviously, then, the visual space of a two-year-old child has already the same particular structure as gives the visual space of adults an upper and a lower side.

On the other hand, further observations seem to show that the difficulty which adults have in recognizing figures in unusual orientations is the outcome of a surprisingly slow and long development. Working under G. E. Müller, F. Oetjen [2] had adults and boys read nonsense texts which were shown in a vertical plane. In this plane the texts had either the normal orientation, or they were turned 90° to the right. Movements of the head were prevented. The times were measured which the subjects spent in reading given amounts of the texts. Under both conditions the children tended to read more slowly than did the adults; but the difference between the reading under normal conditions and that of the turned texts was on the average found to be distinctly smaller in the

[1] Incidentally, Gellermann, who here follows other authors, adopts in his work a criterion of "form perception" which ignores the facts which we are at present discussing. According to this view an animal is capable of form perception if he recognizes a figure independently of its orientation in space. Obviously from this point of view the form perception of adults would be strikingly inferior to that of children.

[2] F. Oetjen, Zeitschr. f. Psychol. 71 (1915), particularly p. 332.

case of the children. This fact assumes particular relevance if we add that the youngest boy was 9 years, the oldest 13½ years old, and that the average age of the (9) children was 11½ years. It seems unreasonable to hold that in this age-class perceptual space is not yet fully structured in terms of vertical and horizontal, above and below. Nevertheless the boys were as a group less disturbed by changed orientation of the texts than were the adults.

Corroborating evidence was found in experiments which R. Mouchly[1] performed under Professor Lewin's guidance. In tables of drawings (outline-pictures of known objects) two pictures were objectively equal. The subjects' task consisted in discovering these equal items among the others when both had the normal orientation, when both were inverted, or when one was inverted and the other in its normal position. The subjects were children between 3 and 4 years, of 5 and of 8 years, and adults. Again the periods of time were measured which the subjects spent in performing these tasks, and it was found that the relative difficulty of the second and the third tasks—in comparison with the first—increased gradually with advancing age. On the youngest children the differences of conditions had practically no influence, but even the children of 8 years were less influ-

[1] Mouchly's results have not been published. I mention them here with Professor Lewin's permission.

enced than were the adults. Thus the dependence of visual recognition on orientation in space is due to a process that seems to extend through many years. Perceptual space, on the other hand, has apparently very early the same directed structure, an upper and a lower side, and so forth, as it has for adults. Under these circumstances I hesitate to believe that the slowly growing influence of spatial orientation on the recognition of figures is actually caused by the directed structure of perceptual space. I even feel inclined to wonder whether we are right in attributing this extremely gradual development to any learning processes.

Obviously more experiments ought to be made on the same problem. The data of both Oetjen and Mouchly may not fully satisfy the statistician, particularly since the rate of this slow development seems to vary considerably from one child to another, and since, on the other hand, not all adults are to the same extent disturbed by changes in the orientation of figures. On the whole, however, these two investigations make it highly probable that the development *is* extraordinarily slow.

We may approach our problem from yet another angle. Is it true that, if we turn a figure in space, its parts merely assume new relations with regard to the right and left, the upper and lower side of space? No thorough study has ever been made of this question; but so far as evidence is available it contradicts the assumption. Figures change in a much more concrete manner when their orientation in space is altered. Many years ago E. Mach pointed out that if we turn a square on edge its appearance differs strikingly from the same objective square when it rests on one of its sides (*cf.* fig. 1). Quite apart from

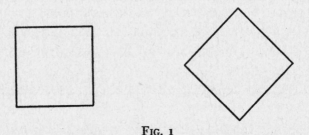

FIG. 1

the fact that in the former orientation the square looks less stable, it also looks much sharper or angular in the sense that its corners seem much more conspicuous. In comparison with it the other square is more of a compact bulk.[1] We owe to E. Rubin[2] the first systematic treatment of what psychologists now call the difference between "figure" and "ground." Objects in visual space, but also circumscribed colored surfaces, and areas which are merely surrounded by a contour, i.e., figures in the widest sense, have as a rule a dense and substantial appearance, while mere ground looks comparatively loose and empty. Figures also tend to stand out in space toward the

[1] For obvious reasons a maximal change will be induced in the square not when it is turned upside down—which yields no change whatsoever—but when it is turned by 45°.

[2] E. Rubin, *Visuell wahrgenommene Figuren* (1921).

subject. Moreover, only figures have, properly speaking, shapes; space between figures is for the most part shapeless. Thus the terms figure and ground refer to an essential perceptual difference. Certain patterns, however, seem at first to be ambiguous in this respect. Either one or another of their parts might be expected to appear as substantial and shaped. Rubin found that in such cases certain rules decide which part will preferably acquire the figure-character. One of these rules says that, if two adjacent areas appear one above the other, and if no other principle interferes, the lower part rather than the upper will be seen as shaped and as substantial. It follows that a change in the spatial orientation of given patterns may lead to a radical alteration in their appearance, inasmuch as parts which were first dense and solid may become loose ground, and vice versa. Among the so-called illusions which have been much studied by psychologists there is one which has an immediate bearing upon our topic. If a figure has two parts, one above the other, which are objectively equal in size, these parts do not as a rule look equal; the lower part appears smaller. It follows that a change in the spatial orientation of figures is likely to alter their proportions. The principle of a further well-known illusion is that the horizontal extension of figures tends to appear shorter than does their vertical size. Resting on its base, for instance, an oblong is not quite so long as it is in the upright position. This is

one more reason why changes in the spatial orientation of figures will tend to alter their proportions and
thus their appearance.

It follows that changes of orientation exert an influence on visual objects which goes far beyond a
mere change of relations between given parts of these
objects and the main directions of space. Further
influences of a similar kind may be discovered in the
future. We see, however, that even those which are
already known, must impede the recognition of
inverted figures.[1]

It is to be regretted that on several occasions which
offered the very best opportunities for observations in
this field no more attention was given to our present
problem. By appropriate devices the projection of the
environment on the retina can be inverted as a whole.
This was first done by Stratton in a classical investigation,[2]
and then by others who varied Stratton's procedure.
Such experiments were meant to solve two problems:
What becomes of visual space under these circumstances?
And what happens to the relations between other sense
departments and motor function on the one hand and
visual space on the other hand? Stratton's report contains
several remarks which refer to actual changes in the characteristics of visual objects after inversion. He says, for
example: "During a walk I was unable to recognize my
surroundings most of the time, although normally they
were quite familiar," and "the objects themselves seemed
strange...." It is quite possible that the optics of the

[1] Some observations indicate that a change of relative position
with regard to left and right tends to influence the appearance of
objects just as does relative position in the vertical dimension.
[2] G. M. Stratton, Psychol. Rev. 4 (1897).

inverting apparatus, the restriction to monocular vision, and similar causes exerted a certain disturbing influence; but in so far as objectively inverted—and therefore now normally projected—objects appeared as normal in this strange experience, observation of the same objects in the objectively upright—but now retinally inverted—orientation might have led to important conclusions. It would have been particularly interesting to know whether or not the strangeness of visual objects tended to disappear at the time at which adaptation of motor functions to the inversion was more or less complete.

If we turn objects upside down we do change their relations to what we call above, below, and so forth. Quite apart from the fact, however, that this does not explain the concrete alterations which objects undergo under such circumstances, there is an extremely simple experiment which proves that changed orientation with regard to those "sides" of perceptual space is not principally responsible for our difficulties in recognizing inverted objects. For this experiment I select a picture, or the outline-drawing of an object, which shows a conspicuous change of appearance when it is turned upside down. This is the case, for instance, with photographs of known or unknown persons. They change so much that what we call facial expression disappears almost entirely in the abnormal orientation. I then ask an assistant to hold this picture behind me and about a foot above the ground in its upright and normal position, while I bend forward until I can see the object between my slightly spread legs. Under these circumstances its retinal image is inverted in comparison with normal retinal projection.[1] Nevertheless the object appears upright, i.e., in its normal orientation with regard to perceptual space. If it is the photograph of a person, the forehead is seen above, the chin below. Under these conditions, therefore, the abnormal position of the image on the retina does not lead to an abnormal orientation of the percept in space. At the same time I see at once that in spite of its upright position the picture has now about the same strange appearance as it has if it is turned upside down, while I look at it from a normal position. A face, for instance, is about as devoid of facial expression as it is in this latter case. In order to complete the experiment I bend once more forward and look backward. This time, however, I ask my assistant to turn the picture upside down. Since my eyes are also turned in space, the normal projection of the picture on the retina is thereby established. But as a visual object the picture now appears inverted; if it is a face the forehead is below in space, the chin above. Nevertheless the strangeness of the picture has now disappeared. I see, for instance, a face which, while it is turned upside down in space, has the normal characteristics of a

[1] Under normal conditions, i.e., if we do not use an inverting device, the retinal image is of course always upside down *in comparison with the object itself,* a fact which has as such no psychological importance.

face, with about the same facial expression as the upright face has when I look at it in the normal fashion.[1]

From this we can draw the following conclusion. Under conditions of normal vision the "sides" of perceptual space, its above and its below, have a fixed relation to definite directions on the retina. For this reason it does not at first seem to matter whether in speaking of the strange appearance of inverted objects we define the abnormal orientation of these objects in terms of perceptual space or in retinal terms. Under the conditions of our simple experiment, however, we find orientation in the former sense separable from orientation in the latter sense. Normal upright orientation in perceptual space can be combined with inversion on the retina, and vice versa. Thus we are enabled to decide in which sense "abnormal orientation" leads to changes in the appearance of objects and to difficulties of recognition. Our observations prove that it is not principally abnormal orientation in perceptual space, but inversion with regard to retinal coordinates, which alters the char-

[1] Printed or written texts cannot be used in this experiment because we read from the left to the right. If a text is held upright but seen in the abnormal bodily position, the words are seen upright, but the (asymmetrical) letters and the sequence of the letters have the wrong direction. This complicates the situation unnecessarily. With a picture, say, of an unknown person there is no such difficulty. Nor is there any difficulty in this respect if we choose a distant mountain-range as an object. And in this case the observation becomes particularly impressive; even the saturation of colors is greatly affected.

27

acteristics of our visual percepts, and thus makes it difficult to recognize these percepts.[1]

For the sake of brevity I have just been contrasting *retinal* orientation with orientation in perceptual space. But I have serious doubts as to whether it is actually retinal orientation on which the characteristics of visual objects depend. Between the retina and those parts of the brain which constitute its main visual center, the so-called striate area, there is an orderly connection so that nerve impulses which originate in a circumscribed part of the retina arrive at a circumscribed part of the visual center. To adjacent regions on the retina correspond in this sense adjacent parts of the visual center. In other words, once the retinal position of an image is given, we know not only about this position but also much about the position and orientation which corresponding processes have in the brain. Thus, when in our experiment we give an image an abnormal orientation on the retina, we change at the same time the orientation of corresponding processes in brain-tissue. It is, I believe, the orientation of such processes in *this* medium which exerts an influence on the characteristics of visual objects and, consequently, on their recognition. As to the nature of this influence merely one remark may be added: The observations which are made in our simple experiment do not

[1] The reader will now realize that in experiments like those which Stratton performed (*cf.* p. 24 f.) the same two points of view must be distinguished.

depend on the particular part of the retina on which the object is projected. In the first form of the experiment the object looks strange, whether we fixate its upper or its lower side; in the second part of the experiment the object has the normal appearance, again independently of such changes of fixation. It is, therefore, not the *place* of retinal projection (and of corresponding processes in the brain) that matters; rather the relation between directions within the object and certain directions within the tissue is the important factor. If this relation is changed, the visual object changes its characteristics. It seems necessary to assume that the tissue of the visual center is permanently pervaded by a gradient which has a fixed direction, and which contributes to the nature of particular processes in this center just as concretely as does the distribution of retinal stimuli in each case. The influence in question seems to become stronger as the individual grows from early childhood to mature age.

That changes in the orientation of objects may lead to difficulties of recognition is about as familiar a fact as is visual movement and its speed. Again, however, mere familiarity does not in this case lead to knowledge of the conditions to which the familiar fact is due. Everybody may realize that an object acquires a new appearance if we turn it into a new position; but, since such changes are localized within the object, and no responsible factor is visible in its environment, no further questions will usually be asked. And yet we have now found that these changes, and consequently the characteristics of visual objects, are partly brought about by a condition which is independent of the objects themselves. Once more psychology is able to reveal functional relationships which remain entirely hidden to everyday experience.

At the risk of fatiguing the reader I have in this case chosen an example which could not be presented in a few sentences, an example whose discussion did not lead to a perfectly clear situation but to a kind of mystery. My intention was to demonstrate convincingly not merely that behind the apparently banal surface of the perceptual world there lie unknown facts of functional dependence, but also that it is sometimes quite as difficult to gain a clear view of these relationships as it is to solve similar tasks in natural science. In the present instance a major difficulty is caused by the fact that we are at first tempted to identify our problem with that of the one-sided directedness of perceptual space. But when this difficulty is overcome we are confronted by the other, that the really responsible factor seems to be inaccessible to psychological investigation.

IV

These two examples will suffice for showing in what sense discoveries are possible in the field of perception. We shall now turn to certain facts of human memory and discuss these facts from the same point of view. Everybody knows that we tend to forget many experiences, or at least the details of these experiences, and there seems to be a general conviction that each content of memory will gradually fade and disintegrate merely because it grows older. Early investigators of memory obviously shared this view. It seemed to them natural to represent their experimental results in terms which show how recall becomes more and more defective the later in *time* the test follows original learning. Time as such was regarded as the principal factor to which the gradual decay of memory traces must be referred.

At present, however, few psychologists will admit that this is an altogether correct assumption. "Curves of forgetting" exhibit certain irregularities. The drop of retention or recall seems to be retarded during intervals of sleep. More particularly it has been shown that, if subjects retire and sleep immediately after learning, retention after 24 hours is better than it is if the same subjects remain awake for a few hours after learning.[1] In 1924 Jenkins and Dallenbach[2] made a special study of this problem. They had their subjects learn certain materials and tested them after 1 or 2 or 4 or 8 hours. During these intervals the subjects either slept or were occupied with their normal day's business. In one respect the former condition

[1] R. Heine, Zeitschr. f. Psychol. *68* (1914).
[2] J. G. Jenkins and K. M. Dallenbach, Amer. Journ. of Psychol. *35* (1924).

would seem likely to yield inferior achievements. The authors report that it was not always easy to arouse the subjects, and that it was difficult to know when they were awake; on the basis of their behavior "it was assumed that they were awake." It stands to reason that under these circumstances the process of recall as such occurred under most unfavorable circumstances. None the less the results were invariably superior when the subjects had been sleeping than they were after an equal interval of daytime activities. As a matter of fact, after the first two hours of sleep the subjects' retention remained constant; they recalled as much after 4 or 8 hours as they did after 2 hours. During the corresponding intervals of waking, forgetting proceeded steadily.

Obviously these results are not in harmony with the view that the mere lapse of time is the main factor which leads to forgetting. Rather they seem related to another fact which was discovered as early as 1900.[1] If, after a learning process, subjects either refrain from work, or undertake further mental activities, a test of retention will yield better results in the first than in the second case, even if the test follows learning after the same time interval. Subsequent mental processes will as a rule impair the retention of previously learned material. This rule, or the concept of "retroactive inhibition," seems to

[1] *Cf.* G. E. Müller and A. Pilzecker, Zeitschr. f. Psychol., Erg.-Bd. *1* (1900).

apply directly to the experimental conditions of Jenkins and Dallenbach. During sound sleep there is, in spite of occasional dreams, probably a minimum of mental activity and therefore of retroactive inhibition. Thus we can see why these authors found that retention is much better during sleep than it is during waking.[1]

Many experiments have been conducted with the purpose of clarifying the nature of retroactive inhibition. Robinson [2] and others have been able to show that retroactive inhibition is the stronger the more closely subsequent processes resemble original learning as to both material and form of activity. This fact has now been established beyond any reasonable doubt. More recently Whiteley [3] discovered the reverse of retroactive inhibition, which we now call "proactive inhibition." Mental work that *precedes* learning will disturb retention just as does subsequent work. In this case again, similarity between the inhibiting and the inhibited processes heightens the degree of the disturbance. This characteristic of proactive inhibition is clearly shown in the following tables which I take from a recent paper of I. Mül-

[1] This explanation may not be complete. It has been shown that mental processes which occur during hypnosis exert little retroactive inhibition on the retention of materials that were learned under normal conditions, and vice versa. It seems possible that the same holds for mental processes which occur during sleep, in their relation to learning before sleep.

[2] E. S. Robinson, The Psychological Monographs 28, No. 6 (1920).

[3] P. L. Whiteley, Journ. of Exper. Psychol. 10 (1927).

ler's.[1] Each table contains the results of a group-experiment. The experimental scheme was the same in both cases.

TABLE I

	1. Group (14 subjects) Preceding series: Syllables	2. Group (13 subjects) Preceding series: Figures
Syllables	U 18 out of 42 = 43%	F 30 out of 39 = 77%
Figures	F 32 out of 42 = 76%	U 18 out of 39 = 46%

TABLE II

	1. Group (55 subjects) Preceding series: Syllables	2. Group (76 subjects) Preceding series: Figures
Syllables	U 105 out of 165 = 64%	F 196 out of 228 = 86%
Figures	F 149 out of 165 = 90%	U 134 out of 228 = 59%

The subjects of both experiments learned and were tested in two groups. Both groups learned the same material, a series of 3 syllables, 3 figures (and 5 numbers, which are of no particular interest in the present connection). After 20 minutes, during which the subjects listened to a lecture, retention was tested (method of free recall). Immediately *before* the learning of the series, however, the two groups of subjects had been occupied with different tasks. One group (1) had learned several short series of syllables (and numbers), the other group (2) the same amount of figures (and numbers). If there was any proactive inhibition, and if its degree depended

[1] I. Müller, Psychol. Forsch. 22 (1937). *Cf.* also H. von Restorff, Psychol. Forsch. *18* (1933).—I reproduce these tables here because proactive inhibition is still a comparatively neglected fact, in spite of its theoretical and practical importance.

34

on the similarity between the inhibiting and the inhibited material, a differential effect was to be expected. The group which was first occupied with syllables should recall the figures of the main series better than the other group which was first occupied with figures. As to the recall of syllables the rôles of the two groups should be the reverse. In the sense of this theoretical expectation the letters F (favorable) and U (unfavorable) are to be understood in the tables. The expectation is fulfilled by the results: In both tables four comparisons between favorable and unfavorable conditions are possible, if we include comparisons within one group of subjects, i.e., for different materials. All eight comparisons show considerably better recall in the favorable than in the corresponding unfavorable condition. Thus proactive inhibition is demonstrated, and at the same time it is proved to depend on similarity in the same way as does retroactive inhibition.

The scientific situation which was thus created was further clarified by experiments of von Restorff's [1] in which it was shown that within one series of materials precisely the same rule holds. It was generally recognized that, if subjects learn one series, say, of syllables, there is again an inhibition, which in this case must be due to interaction among its parts. Von Restorff was able to show that this effect is mainly brought about by the homogeneous character of such a series, in other words, that it depends upon the degree of similarity among the members of the series.

---

[1] H. von Restorff, Psychol. Forsch. *18* (1933). Some experiments of von Restorff's are described in K. Koffka's *Principles of Gestalt Psychology* (1935), pp. 481 ff.—*Cf.* also A. Ortner, Psychol. Forsch. *22* (1937).

Items which differ in kind from the monotonous remainder of the series are much better recalled than are items which belong to this homogeneous part. For obvious reasons the inhibition within one series is stronger than are retroactive and proactive inhibition. Correspondingly the effect of similarity on inhibition is under these circumstances particularly conspicuous. But obviously it is a single identical principle from which all these inhibitions follow. Moreover I. Müller corroborated this unitary view by demonstrating the same effect under conditions in which the distinction between retroactive and proactive inhibition on the one hand, and inhibition within one series on the other hand, becomes quite arbitrary.[1]

It will by now be realized that in the field of memory the situation is very much the same as it is in the field of perception. Forgetting as such is a banal fact; but although common experience makes us acquainted with this fact, it fails to reveal its functional basis. We tend to believe that it is in the nature of each memory trace to become weaker and less accurate simply because it grows older. Psychologists, however, are now inclined to regard this view as much too simple. Their observations indicate "that forgetting is not so much a matter of the decay of old impressions and associations as it is a matter of the

[1] I. Müller, *loc. cit.*, pp. 180 ff. A description of these experiments is given in W. Köhler, *The Place of Value in a World of Facts*, pp. 260 ff. (1938).

interference, inhibition, or obliteration of the old by the new."[1] Since these words were written, proactive inhibition was discovered as a further concrete factor that makes for forgetting. Not merely is the old being obliterated by the new, but apparently also the new by the old. This lends increased plausibility to the theory that forgetting is a matter of disturbing interaction rather than of a deterioration which each trace undergoes independently. At any rate those who believe that independent forgetting in this sense plays the more important rôle have now the burden of the proof.[2]

V

It is not my contention that in psychology facts of functional dependence can be discovered only by indirect procedures. Among our experiences, I repeat, there are many which we may rightly call experiences of specific relatedness and functional coherence. I generally know, for instance, toward what parts of my environment I am directed at a given moment; I often experience how one event grows out of another event; and when I make a statement it expresses a particular relation in which things or concepts actually appear to me at the time. The epistemological importance of such facts cannot easily be over-

[1] J. G. Jenkins and K. M. Dallenbach, *loc. cit.*, p. 612.
[2] The present description of our views in this field is not complete. It fails to mention the factor of *organization* which is most influential both in retention and in forgetting. For the purpose of this chapter, however, our omission is irrelevant.

rated. In fact, it is experiences of this kind which equip such terms as functional dependence with a concrete sense. The indirect inductive procedures of science give us *symptoms* of such a dependence in cases in which it cannot as such be observed. They tell us about regularities of coexistence and sequence. But the methods of science *presuppose* that these regularities may be interpreted as indices of actual causal relationships; and the underlying principle can be justified solely on phenomenological grounds, i.e., by implications which are contained in certain *experiences* of causal relationship.[1] The same experiences serve to give the term functional dependence a definite meaning.

Nevertheless, even such facts must often be considered in a wider context. In other words, understandable relationships may partly depend on further facts in a way that is not fully accessible to direct experience. In such cases the psychologist will once more have to apply his indirect procedures in order to discover the nature of those hidden conditions.

Our attitudes with regard to given objects and occupations may be taken as an example. For the most part we seem to feel that our preferences or aversions are reasonable and legitimate counterparts of the objects or activities to which these attitudes refer.

[1] The import of these remarks will be seen more clearly if I add that regularities of coexistence and sequence do not as such prove any necessity of connection; whereas, conversely, the experience of causation seems to imply regular coexistence or sequence.

And yet there is something in these facts that indicates the presence of hidden influences. Our preferences, if not also our aversions, are subject to what psychologists call satiation.[1] The most beautiful landscape will gradually lose part of its charm if it is seen too regularly; the most interesting occupation will, even in the absence of fatigue, appear less attractive if it is prolonged beyond a certain measure. We are so thoroughly accustomed to the effects of satiation that we may be inclined to regard it as self-evident and as not in need of any further elucidation. But, apart from actual fatigue, there is no obvious reason why prolongation of an attractive activity should make this activity less inviting, or why a view which fascinates us first should no longer do so if we look at it for two hours. Some change is clearly involved which depends upon hidden events. We do not yet know what these events are, and why they have just such an effect. But here again psychology will undoubtedly reveal new important facts of functional dependence.

It seems not to be generally realized that a similar limitation restricts the direct psychological observation of human thinking in so far as it is creative and leads to new insight. The final outcome of the process may be a series of statements which lead in a perfectly sensible sequence to the final end. But among the most important steps of the first creative process

[1] *Cf.* K. Lewin and A. Karsten, Psychol. Forsch. *10* (1928).

39

there is at least one which stubbornly resists an adequate description in purely psychological terms. I will take an example from K. Duncker's interesting experiments on human reasoning.[1] The task is this: Let all numbers like 265265, 837837, 591591 be symbolized as *abcabc*. Why can numbers of this type always be divided by 13? Most people do not find it easy to solve this problem. It is difficult for them to discover any concrete numerical property in the symbol *abcabc* or a common numerical property in the special examples, even if they realize that such a property is what they have to look for. Several attempts will be made to find it; and in a lucky moment the subjects may eventually see that in any number of this type the first three digits give in thousands what the last three give in ordinary units; in other words, that all numbers *abcabc* are at the same time numbers $abc \times 1001$, that they all contain 1001 as a common factor. Once this discovery is made every subject will of course divide 1001 by 13, and will find that 1001 equals 77×13. Thus the problem is solved.—Now, it is extremely unlikely that by mere chance the symbol *abcabc* should be apprehended as $1000 \times abc + 1abc$. If therefore a fair number of persons do solve the problem there must be some positive reason why under these circumstances *abcabc* tends sooner or later to appear in that particular light. I am indeed convinced that the solution

[1] K. Duncker, *Zur Psychologie des Produktiven Denkens* (1935).

occurs rarely, if ever, quite accidentally. On the other hand, I do not see that at this point a continuous sequence of fully understandable conscious processes leads from the problem to this essential step of its solution. To apprehend *abcabc* as *abc* $(1000 + 1)$ is undoubtedly just the right procedure. One realizes this as soon as the step has been taken; henceforth a clear and wholly rational connection leads from *abcabc* to 13. That much insight is, however, impossible so long as the crucial change in the appearance of *abcabc* has not yet occurred. Even if a subject tries hard to transform *abcabc* into something that can be divided by a concrete number, the actual transformation of the symbol *abcabc* will come to him as a pleasant shock, and will thus prove that it was not entirely brought about by a conscious rational process. What happens in such moments? We may be sure that without the subject's continuous efforts in the right general direction the helpful transformation would never occur. It remains none the less true that as psychologists we can not observe why the crucial change occurs at all, i.e., what factors besides our effort are responsible for it; nor can we say why it occurs precisely at the time when it occurs. It follows that in the present case psychologists will once more have to discover certain facts of functional dependence which are not accessible to direct inspection in their experience.

To summarize: Common human experience alone

is not a material with which we can build a science of psychology. Indirect techniques reveal a great many functional relationships by which the contents and the course of mental events are determined. These facts of functional dependence often lie outside the range of direct awareness; and it seems important to realize that even the occurrence of experienced and understandable relationships in emotional life and in thinking is related to factors which are in the same sense but indirectly accessible. It is, I believe, no exaggeration if I say that every psychological investigation without exception will sooner or later reach a stage at which it must try to unearth such hidden functional relationships.

CHAPTER II

The Field of a Percept

"The method which Faraday employed in his researches consisted in a constant appeal to experiment as a means of testing the truth of his ideas, and a constant cultivation of ideas under the direct influence of experiment."

"Faraday sought the seat of the phenomena in real actions going on in the medium."

Clerk Maxwell.

I

At the present time a tremendous amount of psychological work is being done with the purpose of revealing one new fact of functional dependence after another. Thus a number of rules are being discovered which correlate observed events with the factors by which they are determined. We know such rules in the various fields of perception, others that refer to the problems of learning, retention, and recall, and again others which seem to hold in the realm of instincts or needs; there are also tendencies to formulate more general rules which apply not merely in narrowly restricted fields. In fact, the establishment of such rules is the experimentalist's principal business.

I doubt, however, whether in the long run this work can remain self-sufficient. For the most part our

43

rules give us facts of functional dependence which we cannot regard as ultimate and irreducible. Take the very simplest examples: Visual fields tend to be clearly organized in the sense that they contain objects with well-defined boundaries. These objects again tend to appear as parts of larger organizations which we call groups.[1] Proximity and similarity of objects, for instance, are factors which facilitate the organization of objects in group-units. However, strictly psychological methods do not allow us to go any further. We do not learn by psychological investigations in what way, by what functions, these particular factors favor the formation of groups; nor do we see why these rather than different principles hold in visual perception. In the field of memory, we found, interaction among the traces of our past experiences seems to be the most important cause of forgetting. But what does interaction mean in this case? So long as we do not know what mode of existence the traces have which are said to interact, so long, moreover, as we know neither the nature of the interacting forces nor the law which the interaction follows, our statement about the interaction among traces cannot be accepted as the satisfactory solution of a problem. Again—and this is an uncommonly interesting example—Lewin and Zeigarnik have shown that people will more easily recall activities which they were not allowed to complete than others which

[1] *Cf.* M. Wertheimer, Psychol. Forsch. *4* (1923).

they could actually finish.[1] As an explanation it is said that in the first case there remain unreleased tensions which favor the recall of the incomplete tasks, whereas in the second case such tensions naturally disappear when the work is completed. This interpretation is as such very plausible; but it does not completely satisfy our scientific curiosity. When a subject has been occupied with about twenty tasks, and when his work has been interrupted in about one half of these cases, tensions seem indeed to persist which are localized within these incomplete tasks and then make them particularly available for recall. Now, if the tensions survive, the tasks themselves must somehow survive because the tensions are said to refer to the individual incomplete tasks. We shall therefore be interested in knowing what mode of existence we are to attribute to a task when it is no longer a matter of direct experience—for instance, during the subject's occupation with subsequent tasks, and before his attempt to recall the former tasks. This question leads us back to the problem of memory traces. In the present instance, however, these traces assume a special significance by the fact that they contain tensions which facilitate recall. During the period to which I just referred not all these tensions will as a rule be experienced. What then are unexperienced tensions? Everybody will understand what is meant by the term when it

[1] K. Lewin and B. Zeigarnik, Psychol. Forsch. 9 (1927).

applies to work with which the subject is actually occupied; under these circumstances the word tension apparently refers to the subject's self and to his concrete work. But what becomes of this tension at the time when the subject turns to subsequent tasks? Moreover, in what way does the hidden tension help the subject to remember the task to which the tension refers? I have serious doubts as to whether these questions will ever be satisfactorily answered if our thinking remains restricted to psychological concepts. And so long as they are not answered it will be difficult to give this important discovery a clear theoretical interpretation.

It comes then to this: As a rule psychological discoveries refer to facts of functional dependence which are not as such experienced. Thus the rules in which we formulate these relationships imply the occurrence of certain functions in a realm that is surely not the phenomenal realm. As psychologists we cannot say more about this world of hidden existence and hidden functional dependence than is contained in those rules. Therefore the rules themselves tend to sound disappointingly formal and abstract. Psychological investigations alone give us no concrete view of a definite realm of existence within which these rules could actually be understood, interrelated, and derived from general principles. To this extent purely psychological research is not likely to yield a systematic theory of mental facts.

I see only one way in which this difficulty can be overcome. It is now almost generally acknowledged that psychological facts have "correlates" in the biological realm. These correlates, the so-called psychophysical processes, are events in the central nervous system. A given visual field, for instance, is biologically represented by a certain distribution of processes in the occipital lobes of the brain; the correlates of other perceptual facts are located in various other lobes; and many psychological events are likely to concern the brain as a whole.

Although in this manner *all* psychological facts are said to have brain-correlates, we have little reason to believe that, conversely, every phase of brain-activity, the full dynamics of brain-processes, is represented by corresponding phenomenal facts. In other words, the context[1] of brain-events may be wider and functionally more continuous than is apparent in the directly accessible phenomenal situations. We find indirectly, for instance, that a psychological fact A depends on the condition B. But we experience directly merely A and perhaps B, whereas we do not experience their functional interdependence. On the other hand both A and B are represented by certain facts in the central nervous system. If the nervous counterpart of B has an influence on the correlate

[1] I have been unable to discover a satisfactory translation of the German word "Zusammenhang." For the present purpose I shall use the term "context" in this sense. (*Cf.* W. Köhler, *The Place of Value in a World of Facts,* p. 74.)

47

of A, we shall by appropriate psychological procedures find that A depends on B. However, if no experience accompanies that connective brain-event by which the neural counterpart of B exerts its influence upon the correlate of A, it will be only indirect experimental techniques which reveal this functional relationship. Thus we arrive at a psychological rule which expresses a hidden fact of functional dependence. And we shall remain unable to interpret and to understand this fact until our knowledge extends to that particular brain-event by which B actually becomes a condition of A. Within the more complete and continuous context of brain-dynamics a given functional relationship may become concretely understandable, whereas as a mere psychological rule it must be accepted without any further understanding.

Our knowledge of brain-processes is still rudimentary. Thus many believe that for a long time to come psychological rules will have to remain such mere rules, that their translation into a more concrete biological language, and therefore also their systematic causal interpretation, will have to be indefinitely postponed. I do not share this view. On the contrary, it seems to me, our knowledge both of psychological rules and of the nervous system has just reached the stage in which the first bridges can be built from one realm to the other. It will be the psychologist's task to take the first steps in this direction, and we shall next indicate how he will actually have to proceed.

He finds three kinds of material at his disposal: In the first place, the rules of functional dependence which his own work has yielded and is still yielding at a fairly promising rate; in the second place, his knowledge of the nervous system and its functions, which is of course just as modest as is that of physiologists and neurologists; in the third place, his knowledge of those particular parts of physics, physical chemistry, and chemistry which seem applicable to processes in the nervous system.

These materials will be used in the following way. Suppose that by his inductive procedures the psychologist has established a valid rule. According to this rule the occurrence of the psychological fact A depends in the manner R on the condition B. According to our general point of view the rule means that the psychological fact A is associated with a process α in the nervous system, that the factor B is represented by a second state or process β, also in the nervous system, and that A depends on B inasmuch as the physiological fact α depends upon the physiological fact β. R, the formal relationship which the psychologist has established, will then be understood as soon as we become able to interpret it as ϱ, a particular form of physiological or physical interaction between α and β.

In actual fact neither α and β nor ϱ are generally known to us by physiological investigations in the usual sense of the word. If, however, the nature of A and B is compared with all physical and chemical processes which may occur in the nervous system we shall be inclined to associate with A and B definite and particular correlates α and β rather than any others. This choice of α and β will be greatly facilitated by the fact that many physical events will never occur in a medium which has the characteristics of the nervous system.

At the present time the most effective criterion in the selection of physical correlates consists in the principle that, if an experience A may vary in a specific way, its correlate α must be capable of corresponding variations. When consistently applied, this point of view leads to the principle of psychophysical isomorphism.

The same reasoning will apply to ϱ as the biological or physical representative of R. Moreover, once the nature of α and β is hypothetically given, it will be only a few physical relationships between such processes as α and β which can be taken as the concrete biological counterpart of R; because now ϱ must not only be an adequate translation of R in concrete physical terms, it must also be able to establish this relationship between two terms which have the specific properties ascribed to α and β.

If I say that in this fashion a psychological rule can be *understood,* the meaning of understanding is here the same as that of the word explanation in physics.

The occurrence and the characteristics of rainbows, for instance, can be explained if we know some fundamental properties of light on the one hand and of clouds or rain on the other. When seen in this wider context a rainbow is a *necessary* fact. And explanation or theory in this sense remains the principal goal of science, even if it be granted that a few ultimate and general properties of nature will have to be acknowledged which cannot be further explained in the same sense. One advantage of the procedure which I am trying to defend consists in the fact that a psychological relationship R, a fact of hidden functional dependence which is not as such explainable, will by its interpretation as a physiological fact become deducible from general principles of science.

And yet this is but the first step of the procedure. In taking it we introduce hypotheses about the brain-correlates of A and B. Moreover, the physiological interpretation of R as ϱ remains also hypothetical. If we suppose that a theoretically adequate ϱ is actually found, this will give us some confidence in the procedure; because *a priori* no such ϱ might exist, and then our assumptions about the connection of psychological rules with biological facts would prove to be wrong. Nevertheless merely the *possibility* of a theory will in this way be demonstrated. It remains to be shown that our hypotheses point to actual biological facts.

DYNAMICS IN PSYCHOLOGY

A direct verification on strictly biological grounds will often be beyond present technical possibilities. In the meantime an indirect verification which uses psychological techniques may be attempted. Any assumption about the nature of α, β, and ϱ, which is sufficiently specific, will give these entities or processes definite places within the system of concepts with which the natural sciences deal. We are therefore forced to assign to α, β, and ϱ all those characteristics and possibilities of variation which science attributes to these states and events. And there will always be some characteristics and possible variations to which we did not explicitly refer when we selected α and β as correlates of A and B, and ϱ as the concrete biological counterpart of the relationship R. It is at this point that the advantages of biological theory in psychology become particularly striking. When choosing α, β, and ϱ as the physiological correlates of A, B, and R, or in a shorter and more adequate expression ϱ (α, β) as the correlate of R (A, B), we do so in view of a special psychological rule which connects A, B, and R. Generally speaking, however, ϱ (α, β) will be a particular case within a wider body of physical knowledge which comprises besides ϱ (α, β) other particular relationships, say, ϱ' (α', β'). Now, our theoretical procedure does not allow us to make use merely of ϱ (α, β). Implicitly we have decided to accept all the consequences which follow from our hypotheses; and such consequences may extend far beyond the known facts of dependence R (A, B) with which we were at first concerned. Along with ϱ (α, β) we shall be compelled to introduce ϱ' (α', β') into our theory, because in science the former cannot be separated from the latter.

On the other hand, we cannot choose α, β, and ϱ as the biological correlates of A, B, and R without again implying a more general principle of correspondence between psychological data and events in the nervous system. If α, β, and ϱ are the correlates of A, B, and R, then according to this implicit principle of correspondence α', β', and ϱ' must be the correlates of further psychological facts A', B', and R'.

Thus we find, first, that in the system of science ϱ (α, β) implies $\varrho'(\alpha', \beta')$ and, secondly, that according to our principle of correspondence α', β', and ϱ' represent the psychological facts A', B', and R'. Consequently, if we wish to be consistent, we must postulate, *that besides R (A, B) there is another fact of functional dependence R' (A', B'), which lies within the scope of psychological investigation.*

Now, it may be that such a rule has already been independently established in psychology, and that we have been merely unaware of its possible theoretical connection with R (A, B). In this case the known fact of functional dependence R' (A', B') constitutes a partial verification of our physiological theory. It does so even though it may not contain a single biological term. For the most part, however, no such rule R' (A', B') will as yet be known. In this case we shall be under obligation to prepare a situation in which the rule R' (A', B') must show up as a new fact of functional dependence, provided that there actually is such a rule. If we succeed in demonstrating R' (A', B') we thereby verify our hypothesis. And it will be obvious that, although our demonstration may use merely psychological techniques, it means the verification of a *biological* theory. Thus our procedure is psychological in its first part, the discovery of a psychological rule; it then penetrates as theory or hypothesis into the realm of physical nature; and it emerges again into the psychological realm when the consequences of the theory are compared with experimental facts.

I need hardly emphasize that one such indirect verification does not transform the theory into final truth. Other theories, too, might lead to this particular consequence R' (A', B'), and would thus be verified by the same observations. It is merely when one consequence after another is deduced from a theory, and when they are all verified, that we may regard the theory as well-established. Its ultimate verification must of course be direct; physiological tests will eventually have to demonstrate its factual basis. In the meantime we shall greatly profit from such a set of concepts and propositions as will naturally call our attention to new experimental problems. We might never have thought of these without such a stimulating theoretical background. It goes without saying that the experimental tests will not always yield results which agree with the theory. In this case our observations may either contradict the very nucleus of our assumptions or they may militate against an independent minor hypothesis which has been added to this nucleus. The first alternative will force us to choose an entirely new starting point, the latter merely to correct the secondary part of the theory.

II

Our present knowledge of human perception leaves no doubt as to the general form of any theory which is to do justice to such knowledge: a theory of perception must be a *field theory*. By this we mean that the neural functions and processes with which the perceptual facts are associated in each case are located in a continuous medium; and that the events in one part of this medium influence the events in other regions in a way that depends directly on the properties of both in their relation to each other. This is the conception with which all physicists work. The field theory of perception applies this simple scheme to the brain correlates of perceptual facts. In earlier theories of perception such direct mutual influences were but occasionally admitted, and then with so much hesitation that the field principle could scarcely be recognized in those rare theoretical concessions.[1] It was one of the main occupations of Gestalt psychologists to point to one observation after another which proved that the field concept had to be put in the very center of the theory of perception. In the present situation of psychology the great importance of perception lies precisely in this fact, that in perception the acceptance of field concepts has long since become necessary, and that as a consequence it is now becoming a hard task indeed to defend any different views in other parts of psychology.

On the other hand the psychological field theory, it seems to me, is not yet in a satisfactory condition. It still has grave defects in its application both to perception and to other parts of psychology. Its principal short-comings are a certain vagueness and a lack of well-established dynamic principles according to which events in given fields are supposed to be interrelated.[2] Nor can we be surprised by this situation so long as we make no definite assumptions about the medium to which the theory is to be applied, no concrete hypotheses about the nature of the interrelated

[1] The description of the field principle which I here give is itself still too conservative; it sounds too "atomistic." But it suffices for our present purposes.

[2] Professor K. Lewin has recently made great efforts to develop the field theory beyond its first primitive stage. He has tried to achieve this by an analysis of its principal concepts. In the present attempt all stress is being laid on concreteness of our material assumptions about the field. It will be most interesting to see what relation will be found to hold between Lewin's final results and our own.

facts, and none about the actual forces which cause their interrelations. It is the purpose of this chapter to introduce such concrete assumptions.

As a first step in this direction I propose to single out a number of simple observations which will serve to center our program upon one question.

According to von Frey, a touch impression changes its location if at some distance a second such impression is simultaneously given. Since the second stimulus, too, appears shifted toward the first their distance may be strongly decreased. The size of this effect depends upon the intensity of the stimuli.[1]

In vision a similar effect was observed and measured by Scholz.[2] In this case, however, the shortening of the visual distance between the stimuli becomes maximal not when they are simultaneously given, but when the second follows shortly after the appearance of the first.[3] From the physiological point of view, corresponding processes are of course partly simultaneous; but they are not simultaneously in the same state of their development. This condition seems to favor the apparent attraction. Naturally the second stimulus undergoes the greater displacement.[4]

[1] M. von Frey, Zeitschr. f. Biol. *56* (1911) and Psychol. Forsch. *3* (1923).

[2] W. Scholz, Psychol. Forsch. *5* (1924).

[3] E. S. Marks (Journ. of General Psychol. *8* [1933]) describes very neat experiments in which attraction is demonstrated when visual stimuli are *simultaneously* given. (*Cf.* also W. Köhler in *Psychologies of 1930*, ed. by C. Murchison, p. 152 f.)

[4] Scholz found that very short objective distances appeared lengthened rather than shortened. If touch impressions were successively

In the field of hearing, the same phenomenon is at least as striking.[1] Two short noises which have about the same qualitative characteristics appear much too near each other when they are given in rapid succession.

An observation which obviously belongs to the same general class of facts has been well known ever since the first stereoscopes were constructed. The processes of our two eyes are intimately interrelated. The stimulation of a point on one retina gives a visual point which is seen in a particular direction; when stimulating the other eye we can easily find a visual point that is localized in the same direction. "Corresponding points" in this sense have roughly homologous geometrical positions in the two eyes. If in a given position of the eyes two points are stimulated which have precisely corresponding locations, they will be seen as one point. This fusion, however, extends beyond the case of accurate correspondence. As though they attracted each other, two points or lines will fuse in the visual field even though they are projected on slightly "parallactic," i.e., not altogether coresponding, parts of the two retinae. This seems to be a special case of a more general rule. Independently of each other, Spiegel in Germany and

---

given, their distance was shortened (Scholz, pp. 259 ff.); if, however, the objective distance was very short the successively given impressions appeared again too far apart. This held also of successive sounds whose objective distance was small—at least if the time interval was not too short.

[1] W. Scholz, *loc. cit.*, p. 247. P. Kester, Psychol. Forsch. *8* (1926).

Werner in this country made observations according to which, with a greater parallax, the two objects remain separated, but appear *too near* each other. This mutual attraction increases as the parallax decreases; and eventually it results in actual fusion long before the parallax becomes zero.[1]

The apparent attraction which is observed under conditions of *successive* stimulation seems to be related to certain further facts. When given in rapid succession and at some distance from each other two visual stimuli tend to appear as one visual object that moves from the region of the first stimulus toward that of the second. This "stroboscopic" effect is the fundamental fact in all moving pictures. It has played an important rôle in the first development of Gestalt theory.[2] Actual unity, in which any suspicion of the presence of two separate objects is lost, presupposes certain favorable conditions; but even if these are not given, there remains a phenomenon of movement which passes through the area between the stimulated regions. Although this fact is not identical with the apparent attraction which one visual object exerts on another, the stroboscopic effect and the attraction are closely related phenomena. Both depend on the time interval between the first and the second stimulation; and under the same tem-

---

[1] H. G. Spiegel, Psychol. Forsch. *21* (1937); H. Werner, Psychol. Monogr. *218* (1937).
[2] M. Wertheimer, Zeitschr. f. Psychol. *61* (1912).

poral conditions as lead to optimal movement the attraction reaches its maximal amount. In other words, the path of the optimal movement is shorter than is the phenomenal distance between the stimuli for any greater or smaller time interval.

The stroboscopic movement exhibits a further characteristic which lends increased interest to these observations. In one of his papers Professor Wertheimer[1] describes an experiment on stroboscopic movement in which this effect is shown to depend upon the particular characteristics of the stimuli in question. If short exposure of an object is closely followed by the exposure of two objects of the same kind and at equal distances from the first, a movement toward both will often be seen. If, however, the first object and one object of the subsequent pair are alike as to color, size, and shape, while the other member of this pair differs strongly from those two, the movement will preferably pass through the area between the equal objects.

At this point we are reminded of a basic fact in the perceptual organization of *stationary* objects, which has once before been mentioned. Suppose that a number of objects are shown at equal distances from each other. In spite of this regular distribution specific groups will be formed if some of the objects

1 M. Wertheimer, Psychol. Forsch. *4* (1923), pp. 314 f. For a more particular analysis and special conditions *cf*. P. von Schiller, Psychol, Forsch. *17* (1933), pp. 188 ff.

have a property in common and differ thereby from the others. In the following example, for instance, which is a variation of one of Wertheimer's figures,[1] we see one pattern of dots as vertical lines, the other pattern as horizontal lines. (*Cf.* figs 2A and 2B.)

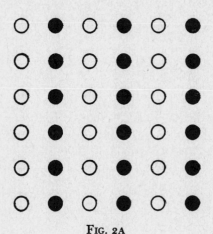

FIG. 2A

Like dots unite in both figures so that groups are formed which appear in one case as vertical and in the other as horizontal lines. Thus in these stationary patterns the same principle of likeness operates as was just found to influence the direction of stroboscopic movements.

From all these facts we shall now draw our first theoretical conclusions. In the first place it is not the self or any mental processes which bring about those

[1] M. Wertheimer, Psychol. Forsch. *4* (1923), p. 309.

apparent attractions in several sensory departments, the stroboscopic movement with its peculiarities, and the grouping of objects with its dependence on the factor of similarity.[1] It is true that changes of mental attitude *may* influence these phenomena just as they

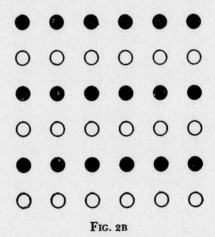

FIG. 2B

may exert a certain influence on other facts of organization. Normally, however, even a passive observer will find that those distances are too short, that the stroboscopic movement prefers the path between like objects, and that specific groups tend to include similar objects rather than heterogeneous

[1] Recently I. Krechevsky has argued that without any particular need no specific grouping will occur in the visual field of a rat. He also supports this view by most interesting experiments. *Cf.* I. Krechevsky, Journ. of Exper. Psychol. 22 (1938). It may be, however, that in these experiments the objective conditions for specific grouping were not present in such a degree as to suffice for spontaneous grouping in the case of the rat.

material. Therefore we are here dealing with facts
of *sensory* organization.

In the second place, I repeat, the observer is unaware of the way in which the presence of a second
object displaces a first, and vice versa. He does not
experience in what manner two successively given
stimuli co-operate in producing a stroboscopic movement; nor does he see why likeness of these stimuli is
a favorable condition for its occurrence. Again, he
may recognize that likeness among several objects
favors their appearance as one group; but he cannot
tell us for what reason likeness has this particular
effect.

To the extent, therefore, to which these observations bear witness to an interaction which cannot
as such be observed within the phenomenal realm,
they cannot be understood in purely psychological
terms. According to our general program we shall
therefore assume that the interaction occurs among
the brain correlates of the perceptual facts in question.

Let us first consider the case of apparent attraction, for instance, in the field of touch. Two points
on the forearm of a subject, perhaps 10 cm. apart,
are simultaneously stimulated, and their distance appears much smaller than corresponds to their localization when they are singly given. We have good reasons to assume that the brain correlates of these
stimuli are located in the posterior central gyrus. If

the stimuli are separated by a considerable distance on the skin of the arm, their correlates will also have separate locations in the posterior central gyrus. The fact, however, that both stimuli appear as displaced toward each other can be due only to an influence which the neural counterpart of the first exerts on that of the second, and vice versa. It must be this influence which alters the localization of the points in phenomenal space.

Under these circumstances we shall have to ask ourselves in what manner the brain correlate of one stimulus can have any effect on the brain correlate of a second stimulus, if the locus of the former is different from that of the latter. The same question will arise if apparent attraction is considered not in the field of touch but in vision and in hearing. Whatever may be the more particular conditions on which the displacements depend in these cases, there are such displacements, and they involve the same problem.

We shall be better prepared for an answer if the nature of the problem is first more fully realized. It will be obvious that the stroboscopic movement and the grouping in visual space require an explanation in terms of interaction just as do the facts of apparent attraction. Both in the stroboscopic movement and in perceptual grouping, however, the concrete characteristics of the stimuli are found to play a selective rôle. Interaction depends in these cases on the relation which obtains between the properties of the interacting processes. Our question will therefore assume this form: How can the neural correlates of separate and distant stimuli influence each other in a way that depends upon the relation between their particular characteristics? I see no more than one way in which such facts can be explained. A process α cannot determine what happens to a distant process β (and vice versa) unless the presence of α is somehow represented at the locus of β (and vice versa). Moreover, this influence cannot be specific unless the representation of one process at the locus of the other is equally specific; in other words, unless not merely the presence of a process in general but also its concrete properties are to a degree represented in the surrounding tissue.

These remarks must sound familiar to those who are acquainted with the history of physics. One hundred years ago Faraday began, against the ideas of his time, to speak of the *field* around a charged body not as a mathematical fiction but as a fundamental physical fact. "He sought the seat of the phenomena in real actions going on in the medium."[1] If other things are at a distance influenced by the presence of that first object, this effect, he said, must be due to the presence of the *field* of the object at the distant locus

[1] C. Maxwell in the Preface to *A Treatise on Electricity and Magnetism*. In Maxwell's statement "phenomena" is of course a synonym of *physical* facts.

of its action. Our examples show that in the theory of perception we are now in precisely the situation in which Faraday found himself when he investigated electrostatic, electromagnetic, and electrodynamic interactions. If an attempt is made to give an interpretation of those perceptual facts in terms of brain function, it will be advisable to follow Faraday's example.

The first and most essential assumption which we shall have to introduce for this purpose is clearly implied in our last argument. If in a certain sense the correlate of a percept may be said to have a circumscribed local existence we shall none the less postulate that as a dynamic agent it extends into the surrounding tissue, and that by this extension its presence is represented beyond its circumscribed locus. There is no contradiction in these statements. So far as certain properties of the percept process are concerned, this process may be confined within a restricted area, and with this nucleus the percept itself may be associated as an experience. At the same time the presence of such a percept nucleus may lead to further events in its environment, of which we are for the most part not directly aware; but this halo or field of the percept process may be responsible for any influence which the process exerts upon other percept processes.

In this way the problem of perceptual interaction becomes first of all a problem in the theory of *single*

66

percepts. It should, however, be emphasized at once that the interpretation of the perceptual field will not for this reason assume a merely summative form. To a single percept in an homogeneous environment we attribute its field; another percept, given elsewhere in absence of the first, would also have its independent field; but from the point of view of physics it seems unlikely that, when both are present, the field of the pair should be merely the superposition of the fields of its members taken singly.

The first clear indication of similar views will be found in Wertheimer's investigation of stroboscopic movement.[1] At the present time, it seems to me, we can give the field concept in psychology a more specific physical content.

III

We shall now leave the problem of interaction aside; or, more correctly speaking, we shall temporarily appear to do so; because actually we shall return to it almost at once. At any rate we shall now try to develop a plausible hypothesis about the nature of single percepts.

Stationary visual percepts, a tree, a stone, or a book, are as a rule extremely reticent as to the nature of the neural events which underlie their existence. We may hope to learn more about brain correlates if we turn to instances in which percept

[1] M. Wertheimer, Zeitschr. f. Psychol. *61* (1912).

processes seem to be in a more active state. This is the case with "reversible figures." The example which is here given (fig. 3) has now a certain fame owing to Rubin's investigation of "figure" and "ground." [1]

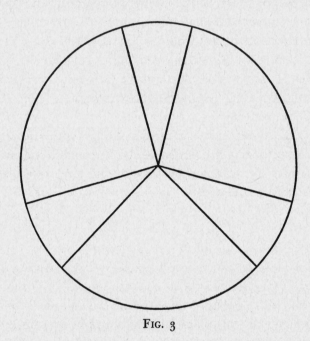

When the center of this pattern is fixated it will after a while be suddenly transformed. If, for instance, the three narrow angles—in our example angles of 30°— were first seen as a figure, and the large angles as part of the background, after a sudden change the latter

---

[1] E. Rubin, *Visuell wahrgenommene Figuren* (1921).

will constitute the figure, and the former will recede into the background. Soon this configuration will again be replaced by the first, and so forth. Thus a sequence of abrupt transformations will be observed which, I believe, no subject is able to prevent.[1] With new subjects knowledge of the two configurations seems to have a certain influence on the speed of the changes; i.e., once they are acquainted with the second possibility, this second organization will more easily replace the first. In a short time, however, the curious behavior of the pattern will become quite reliable in the sense that it will be repeated if the same conditions are once more given. For purposes of measurement it is advisable to prescribe a constant attitude of the subject. I find it convenient to ask observers to "keep" whatever figure they may see at a given time. Greatest care should be taken with regard to many conditions upon which the behavior of the pattern strongly depends. Several drugs, but also visual factors in the environment, influence the rate of the changes tremendously.

If the reversals are registered it will be found that, as the time of observation increases, the changes tend to follow each other more rapidly. After a while, however, the reversals will become less "orderly"; they may, for instance, occur in one part, but not

---

[1] W. Köhler, *Gestalt Psychology* (1929), pp. 185 f. As Graham has shown, the behavior of reversible figures follows quantitative rules. *Cf.* C. H. Graham, Journ. of General Psychol. 2 (1929). My own observations agree with those of Graham.

at the same time in the remainder of the figure. With some subjects it is possible to overcome this difficulty by interrupting the observation for certain periods, and to measure the rate of the reversals for limited stretches, say, for 5 complete cycles of the process.[1] I give here the curves which were thus obtained from two subjects (fig. 4). Times for 5 complete cycles are plotted against successive periods of observation. As the graph shows, the time for 5 cycles decreases as the number of observation periods increases; i.e., the reversals follow each other more and more quickly. (In these experiments the periods of observation were interrupted by rest intervals of one minute each.)

I am by no means in a position to give an actual theory of the reversals as such, least of all since with many subjects the figure does not show the same regular behavior. In fact, these experiments are here mentioned merely because they first suggested a simple hypothesis about the nature of percept processes: Prolongation of continuous observation—with constant fixation of the center—tends to decrease the average time during which the figure will stay in a given part of the pattern; repetition of observation periods tends to have the same effect. These facts point to the possibility that prolonged occurrence of a figure process in a given area leads to gradual

---

[1] The fifth cycle is completed when the first figure appears for the sixth time, including its appearance in the beginning.

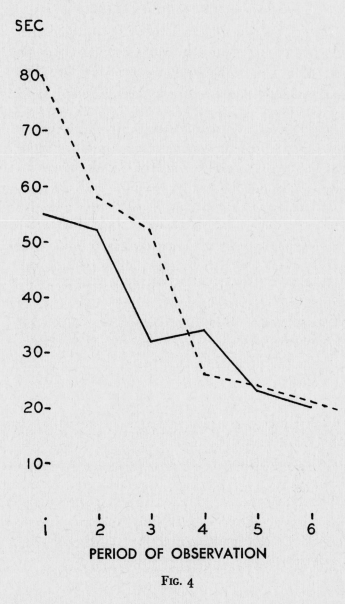

SEC

PERIOD OF OBSERVATION

FIG. 4

changes in this area which oppose the further existence of the process in the same place; in other words,
a figure process seems to have some effect by which
it tends more and more to block its own way. Moreover this effect seems to persist beyond the time
during which the figure process actually occurs; it
may not completely disappear in a minute or more,
and thus with repeated observation a progressively
stronger after-effect will be obtained by summation.

This assumption can be tested in the following
manner. Owing to the factor of proximity, which
favors the formation of narrow rather than wide
visual units, the narrow angles are on the average
seen longer as a figure. We shall therefore expect the
effect of prolonged observation to be stronger within
the narrow angles and to be much weaker, say, in the
middle of the wider angles. Consequently, if the pattern is first made unstable by repeated observations,
and if it is then turned by about 60°, it should once
more become more stable, the rate of reversals slower.
I made this experiment many times with subjects
whose "curves of blocking" were of the clear and reliable type shown in the graph (fig. 4). In its new
position the figure was always much more stable
than it had been immediately before the change,
although it proved to be slightly less stable than it
was in the same position if no previous blocking had
occurred.

This is not a real proof of our assumption, particularly because such experiments cannot be performed with all subjects. Nevertheless the hypothesis seems to deserve further thought. First of all we will make it more concrete. Do any known processes tend to alter the medium in which they occur, and thereby to block their own path? The processes in question would have to be of such a kind as to fit the general physical conditions which prevail in the nervous system, and also the particular circumstances which are given in the present case. It is easy to find a process that fulfills these requirements. On the other hand I cannot find more than one such process. Electric currents in electrolytes change all interfaces in their path through which the ions of those solutions cannot pass freely. This holds no less for electrolytical conduction in organic tissue than it does for currents in inorganic solutions. The effect is especially strong in the tissue because this medium includes so many cells whose boundaries constitute interfaces. The primary effect that occurs at interfaces is an accumulation or rarefication of ions. These changes of ionic concentration may, however, have many secondary effects. There will be adsorption of ions on the interfaces, electromotive forces will here originate which are opposed to the direction of the current, chemical reactions may take place, local resistances may be heightened, the permeability of the interfaces themselves may be altered. In the nervous system there may be still further effects, which we cannot yet define in purely physical terms. In this respect we need not make any special hypotheses. We shall merely assume that currents which are conducted in the tissue tend to alter this medium, and thereby to impede their own further passage. With this postulate general physiological experience is in complete agreement.

We are interested in the nature of percept correlates as such. From this point of view the spontaneous transformations of some special patterns are significant merely in that they point to one particular characteristic of those correlates. Percept processes here show a behavior which is obviously analogous to that of currents in electrolytes. Can it be that percepts are actually associated with electric currents in the nervous system?

The present situation in nerve physiology makes this assumption quite plausible. We shall see this as soon as we consider recent discoveries concerning the transmission of nerve impulses from one neuron to another, and from a neuron to a gland or a muscle fiber. Primarily these discoveries refer to the autonomic division of the nervous system. They give convincing proof of the fact that nerve impulses do not as such pass from one neuron to another or to an effector. Rather, when an impulse arrives at the end of a fiber, a chemical substance, a neurohumor, is here secreted into the surrounding medium. Upon reaching other neurons or an effector it stimulates these further organs. We know that there are several such neurohumors.[1]

It has not yet been decided whether in the central nervous system the arrival of a nerve impulse at the end of a fiber has similar chemical effects. Several physiologists, however, seem to regard it as unlikely that in this respect the two divisions of the nervous system differ essentially.[2] We shall therefore assume that, when nerve impulses arrive at the end branches of sensory fibers, chemicals penetrate from the fibers into the common medium which here surrounds those branches. Nerve impulses, we know, are *waves* of activity. Moreover, in its normal state a particular fiber will always conduct waves of a given intensity, if it conducts at all. This intensity of the impulse does not vary when the intensity, with which the fiber is stimulated, varies. But with increasing intensity of stimulation the *number of waves*, which pass through the fiber per unit of time, will grow within certain limits. Furthermore, a small area of the sensory surface is in functional connection not with one but with several fibers. The threshold of excitation varies from one fiber to another. It follows that, with increasing intensity of stimulation, a greater number of fibers will be activated in such a common area, and that

[1] G. H. Parker, *The Origin, Plan and Operational Modes of the Nervous System* (1934); W. B. Cannon and A. Rosenblueth, *Autonomic Neuro-Effector Systems* (1937).

[2] A. Forbes in *Handbook of General Experimental Psychology* (1934), pp. 176 ff. W. B. Cannon and A. Rosenblueth, *loc. cit.*, pp. 55-58.

thus the *density of active neurons* within the area will become a second variable of nervous conduction which corresponds to the intensity of peripheral stimulation.

In this description of nerve conduction in sensory fibers there are two factors which may at first appear puzzling. In the first place, the nature of our percepts does not hint at any discontinuity in the processes with which they are associated. In the second place, percepts exhibit as a rule not two but merely one variable, which is correlated with the intensity of peripheral stimulation. Both difficulties disappear, however, if we assume that the primary effect of nerve impulses in ganglionic layers, for instance in the cortex of the brain, consists in chemical activity. Chemicals (neurohumors) which are secreted by the ends of the fibers will tend to disappear by diffusion, and by reactions with other materials. If, however, impulses follow each other with sufficient speed, their chemical effects will overlap in time, and soon a stationary state will be reached in which the chemical in question will be replaced at the same rate at which it tends to disappear. Thus in ganglionic layers there will be a stationary state in spite of the fact that the nerve messages are discontinuous. The level of this stationary state will depend on the frequency with which the impulses arrive in individual fibers, i.e., on the intensity of peripheral stimulation. At the same time the stationary state will depend upon the

number or density of all active fibers whose inter-
mingled end branches feed this particular region;
i.e., it will again depend upon the intensity of peripheral stimulation. Thus the dual representation
of intensity in nerve conduction will become a
unitary effect of intensity in those parts of the brain
in which nerve conduction is transformed into chemical activity.

If these premises be accepted, we are immediately
led to certain conclusions about the nature of
percept processes. Suppose that on the retina a white
circle or any other figure is projected, and that its
environment is a uniform gray. In this case neuro-
humoral action in the visual center of the brain will
assume the following form. In the circumscribed area
which corresponds to the white retinal figure, impulses will arrive at a high frequency and in many
individual fibers; in this area chemical activity will
therefore be maintained at a high level. In the
environment, on the other hand, where fewer impulses arrive in a smaller number of active fibers,
the level of chemical activity will be lower. Thus, if
we disregard the effects of retinal fatigue, two *stationary* chemical processes will occur side by side.
They remain stationary inasmuch as all materials
which participate in the reactions are kept at constant levels of density or concentration. Therefore
the presence of two different but adjacent processes
is tantamount to the presence of two different but

adjacent chemical media or "phases." [1] It is hardly a special assumption if we postulate that ions take part in those chemical processes. To a given process we shall therefore have to attribute a certain concentration or density of participating ions.

From this point of view the area which corresponds to the white figure contains certain ions in one concentration, and the area which corresponds to the gray environment contains these ions in another concentration. Since both areas lie in the common medium which surrounds fibers, dendrites, and cell bodies, they have a free common boundary in the sense that ions in minute quantities can diffuse from the zone of higher concentration into that of lower concentration. This will occur at once, and as a consequence one of the areas will become electropositive, the other electronegative with reference to its neighbor. In this manner an electromotive force will be established between the figure and its environment. [2]

For very simple reasons a single electromotive force between two chemical phases cannot give rise to a closed and stationary current. The two areas will, however, be in contact with other parts of the tissue, with cell boundaries and so forth, which from the point of view of physical chemistry constitute a

---

[1] The term is here used in the meaning given to it by W. Gibbs.
[2] For the theory of these forces *cf.* W. Nernst, *Theoretische Chemie,* or any textbook of physical chemistry.

further phase. At the common boundaries of this third phase with both the figure and its environment, further electromotive forces will arise.[1] Thus a situation will be established which we may represent by a simple scheme (fig. 5):

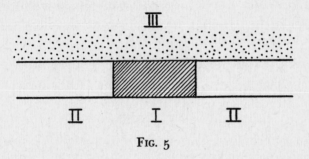

I is the area of the figure, II that of the uniform environment, III is adjacent tissue. The scheme shows a cross section of the situation in two dimensions.

There will be electromotive forces at the boundary I/II at which the figure and the environment are in touch, at the boundary II/III of the environment and adjacent tissue, and at the boundary III/I of the neighboring tissue and the figure. These three forces can maintain a current which will spread from the figure (I) into its environment (II), from here into the adjacent tissue (III), and then back into the figure. The intensity of this current will depend on the brightness difference between the figure and its

[1] *Cf.,* for instance, R. Beutner, *Die Entstehung elektrischer Ströme in lebenden Geweben* (1920), pp. 47 ff.

environment. If the figure is small or of moderate size, the density of electric flow will be highest within the area of the figure; outside the figure the current will spread more widely, and thus its density will be lower; at any rate, however, it will envelop the figure completely. I should perhaps mention that it will not flow along particular conductors; rather it will pervade the tissue as a continuous macroscopic process.

This is the simple model of a percept process which I propose to use in the field theory of perception. It realizes the suggestion that electric currents accompany the occurrence of percept processes. Moreover, it fulfills the postulate that a percept process is represented beyond its own locus in a narrower sense. For in this scheme the figure itself remains a circumscribed area, and yet the current which passes through this area pervades the environment at the same time. Since it is the presence of the figure which causes this current we are justified in saying that its flow constitutes a functional halo or *field* of the figure. It was our intention to explain the fact that percepts seem to interact over distances. This, we assumed— and here we followed Faraday—is possible only if a single percept has a field. And we realize now that the field of a percept is due to its interaction with its immediate environment, i.e., to the fact that the very nature of a percept process involves a functional relationship with its surroundings.

THE FIELD OF A PERCEPT

In a way the present theory postulates two physical factors which both represent a given percept beyond its own locus. If a current flows through and around a percept-area it can do so merely because the medium is pervaded by electrostatic forces which are derived from the electromotive forces at the boundaries of the phases. As a matter of fact the distribution of the current corresponds everywhere to that of those electrostatic vectors. Forces and electric flow are in this sense inseparable. We shall, however, be more strongly interested in the current because it is an action of the current which we can test in the following psychological experiments.

In many respects we have not yet completed the theory. I will mention merely one point at which it will soon have to be amplified. The field around a percept announces not only the presence of this percept; we have seen that it also represents its specific characteristics. Now it is obvious that the distribution of the current around a percept process depends directly upon the shape of the percept itself. But surely interaction between percept processes is influenced by other properties of these processes besides their shape. Thus a percept field must also represent these further properties. The theory will not be acceptable unless it can explain this fact. I prefer, however, to postpone the discussion of such problems until the most direct consequences of our assumption have been tested.—

The theory contains, first, the hypothesis that percept processes are associated with currents through and around the percept-nucleus; secondly, a more special assumption about the electromotive forces which drive these currents through the tissue. It might be doubted whether the derivation of these electromotive forces is already correct in every detail. Indeed in this respect certain modifications of our scheme may sooner or later become necessary. On the other hand, it is a well-known fact that any local excitation in the nervous system gives rise to electromotive forces between this particular region and its environment. Thus there is little speculation in our assumption that a percept process must be pervaded and surrounded by electric flow; this assumption will stand even if the more special hypothesis about the electromotive forces involved should prove to be in need of minor alterations.

IV

In the beginning of this chapter I remarked that perceptual facts do not generally reveal *why* they depend on certain factors. I concluded that the *dynamics* of many perceptual processes in the brain has no phenomenal counterpart, in other words, that merely its effects are perceived; and that for this reason a satisfactory functional interpretation of perception can be given only in terms of biological theory.

For the most part the field around a percept is indeed not directly observable. For this reason we are unable to test the present theory by any simple inspection of percepts. There is, however, an indirect way in which the theory can be tested. In fact this way is actually prescribed by our explanation of the behavior of reversible figures. This explanation assumed, in the first place, that prolonged occurrence of a percept process in a given area changes the medium in which the process is located, and that it does so gradually and continuously. To this we added the second assumption that, when the change has reached a certain critical degree, the reversible pattern is suddenly transformed.

Only one of these hypotheses, the second, refers to the special behavior of reversible figures. The first states something about gradual effects of percept processes in general; its import is not restricted to any particular class of percepts. What indeed are reversible figures? They are ordinary percepts in every respect except that they contain the possibility of two distributions of figure and ground which can alternate. Therefore, if any other percept be given for prolonged inspection, the corresponding brain process should alter its medium just as does the process of a reversible figure. This change may not lead to a sudden transformation. But it would be astounding if it did not show in any way whatsoever.[1] We are thus led to ask in what respect, if in any, an "old" percept differs from a "fresh" one.

I shall now describe a number of very simple observations. They are meant to answer the very first questions which arise from our theoretical scheme; and their significance will be understood without any difficult theoretical deductions.

In simple observation it is for the most part hard to say whether the appearance of a visual percept changes with prolonged inspection. But it is easy to decide whether, after prolonged presence, such a

[1] This holds of course whether or not we regard the percept process as associated with an electric current.

percept looks different from a second objectively equal figure, which is still "young." It will be advisable to choose for this comparison not fully colored surface figures, but patterns of which merely the outer contour is given. Surface-figures give strong after-images which would disturb the observation. Thin black contours on a white ground, however, give weak after-images; as a matter of fact, for many people they give no perceptible after-images at all.

The current-theory of percepts will in this case assume a particular form. We have to expect that the current passes on the one hand from the contour into the interior, from the interior into the third medium (*cf.* above p. 79), and from this medium back into the contour; on the other hand, it must flow from the contour into the environment, from the environment into the third medium, and from this medium back into the contour. Thus the current will consist of two parallel branches, an inner and an outer circuit. Its density will be highest in the contour, because here it passes through a very narrow space; the density will also be comparatively high in the interior of the figure, because this area again offers a fairly narrow passage; and it will be less dense in the wider environment, particularly at a considerable distance from the figure.

1. On a large piece of white cardboard two equal rectangles are drawn with India ink. So long as these

figures are not too large it does not matter what
special relation obtains between their edges. On the
other hand, the oblongs should not be too near each
other. In the middle between these rectangles a fixation point is given (fig. 6). When this point is fixated
from a distance of a few yards the figures look alike.
One of them is now covered with a white screen and
the point is fixated for some time. Three minutes
will generally suffice, but with some observers a

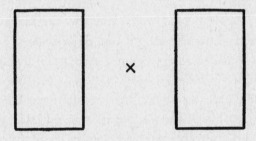

FIG. 6

longer time may give more convincing results. When
after this period the screen is removed, and the second oblong becomes visible, the two figures no longer
look alike. The old figure is smaller, it lies farther
back in space, and its contour is pale in comparison
with the deep black of the other figure. All subjects
make this third observation; for many, the difference
in size is quite as striking, but some describe the
depth-effect as the most impressive difference between the two rectangles.

This simple effect shows merely that prolonged inspection changes a percept in *some* way; it does not tell us what kind of a process is responsible for the change. Moreover, at least the paleness of the old contour in comparison with the new could easily be explained by retinal fatigue. And one might suspect that both the change in size and the depth-effect are mere by-products of the same banal factor. For this reason conditions are changed in the next observation.

2. The same pattern is used, and the same point is fixated, while the second oblong is covered by the screen. But now merely one eye sees the first figure. (Certain facts, which we need not here describe, make it inadvisable to *darken* the second eye. One can easily hold one hand before it in a way that makes the figure invisible and yet admits light into this eye.) After some minutes of steady fixation the rôle of the eyes is reversed, and the screen is removed at the same time. It will now be observed that the "old" figure exhibits approximately the same changed appearance as it did in the first experiment, although in this test it is seen by an eye into which this figure was not projected during the period of prolonged fixation.

It follows that the factor of retinal fatigue has no essential connection with these observations. It becomes probable, moreover, that the effect is located in the brain, where processes which are due to stimulation of corresponding parts of the two retinae occur in a common area.

For obvious reasons the second experiment should not be made immediately after the first. The after-effects of prolonged inspection will often persist for several minutes, particularly if the inspection period itself has been long. The same warning applies to the following observations. They have to be kept apart from each other in time.

3. Once it is known what particular phenomena we are to observe, experimental conditions can be chosen in such a way as to test the validity of our theoretical scheme. First of all, if it is a percept-*current* which gives rise to those changes, its effects should not be confined to the contours. They should, for instance, appear in the *interior* of a contour-figure where the white of the cardboard differs in no perceptible way from that outside the figure. Here, the theory states, the density of the current, and therefore its effect, must be quite strong. This consequence can be tested together with a second deduction from the theory, namely, that within certain limits[1] the after-effects of prolonged inspection should be observable, whatever particular object we use in the tests. This follows from the fact that, once a current has altered the medium through which it flows, this medium will be in a changed condition

[1] *Cf.* below, p. 98.

87

for any other current which passes through parts of the same medium. For this purpose the next experiment was designed.

A single black circle is shown on the white ground. The fixation point lies below the periphery of the circle. After the inspection period this pattern is covered by another large white surface on which two squares are visible symmetrically above and below a fixation mark. When this point is fixated the upper square lies precisely in the middle of the area which was before surrounded by the circle, and the lower square lies far away from this area (fig. 7).

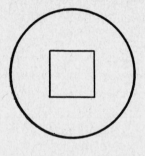

FIG. 7

THE FIELD OF A PERCEPT

In the figure the position of the test pattern—thin lines—is indicated within the inspection field. Actually the circle is not visible during the test. The test objects, on the other hand, are absent during the inspection period; moreover, their contours are just as thick as is the circle; they are here shown in thin lines merely for the purpose of making it easier to distinguish them from the inspection pattern. In this particular experiment the radius of the circle may, for instance, be 2 centimeters, the distance between its center and the fixation mark $3\frac{1}{2}$ centimeters, and the edge of the squares $1\frac{1}{2}$ centimeters. Somewhat different measures, however, would not give essentially different results.

When the inspection pattern is replaced by the test pattern the upper square appears smaller than the lower square. For some subjects it also lies clearly back in space, and its color is gray in comparison with the black of the lower square.

I once made this experiment with a group of seven subjects none of whom knew anything about the theory or about the fact which the experimenter expected them to observe. They were merely asked to write what they had to say about the appearance of the squares. On the other hand, I lengthened the inspection period to 8 minutes in order to cause a strong effect which these completely naïve observers would not miss. All seven subjects reported that the upper square was smaller than the lower one. The squares had equal sizes when seen under normal conditions.

This is the first observation which directly concerns the theory. An after-effect in a less particular sense might be restricted to the contours. In the present observation, however, it is shown that a white area which is objectively just as homogeneous as the ground outside the figure, assumes strongly altered functional properties when, for a considerable time, it is the figure area within a given contour. Some may still have a suspicion that the difference between figure and ground is somehow brought about by learning; that its origin is indirect, not visual. Our experiment seems to exclude this interpretation; because it shows that the area which has been a figure for several minutes differs afterwards in a concrete functional way from another visual region which has been mere ground. The current-theory, on the other hand, gives a direct explanation of this fact. Inside the figure area the current must have a very high density because it cannot spread freely, and its altering effect upon the medium must be correspondingly strong. The lower test object, it is true, lies in a region through which some part of the outer current may pass; if it does, its effect will at any rate be much less intense, because here the density of flow must be lower. Thus the difference in the appearance of the squares is explained.

Quite apart from this the outcome of the present experiment opens the way for a much wider range of further tests. It shows that we can put test objects in any part of a visual field in which we are interested, and that we can thus observe how these parts are influenced by prolonged inspection of a given figure. From the point of view of the theory we can in this manner explore the distribution of the current or field in and around that percept.

4. We have just remarked that the outside current will spread more widely than does the inside current. The corresponding difference in density leads to strong differential effects in the appearance of test

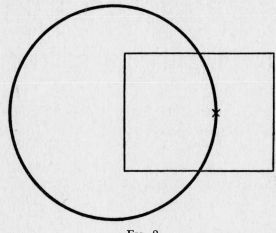

FIG. 8

objects which lie just inside and outside the contour of a given figure. In the next experiment we again take a circle as the figure;[1] the fixation point lies on the periphery at the height of the center. The test objects have the form of a rectangle which is divided by a curve. This curve is congruent with the corresponding part of the circle, and the fixation mark of the test pattern lies in the middle of this curve.

[1] It might of course be any other figure.

(Fig. 8 must be interpreted in the same way as fig. 7. The contours of the test pattern are not thinner lines; the circle and the test pattern are not simultaneously given.[1])

After the inspection period (8 minutes) all subjects report that the right side of the test-oblong is clearly larger, and that it stands out in space. It deserves to be mentioned that under ordinary circumstances just the opposite depth effect will generally be seen. Before the inspection period the subjects have been shown this test object. They all have agreed that its *left* side appears as a figure which lies somewhat in front of the right side. There is indeed a tendency for convex rather than concave areas to assume the figure character. After the inspection period, however, this relation is inverted. The convex area lies behind the concave area, because the former falls within a region which the figure process has more strongly altered.[2] There is, however, something in the present observation that surprises all subjects. The sizes of the two test-areas do not merely appear as clearly different. They actually differ so strongly that the straight horizontal contours are broken. Where the outlines of the outer and the inner area are in contact the inner area joins the outer area in the manner indicated in fig. 9.

[1] This also holds for all further experiments which are here reported.
[2] At this point the connection between the present experiments and those on reversible figures becomes apparent.

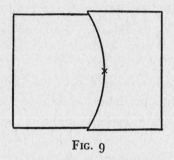

FIG. 9

5. In none of these experiments have we yet tried to demonstrate an effect *outside* the figures. What has been shown is merely that the size, the location in the third dimension, and the brightness of test objects *within* figures are altered in comparison with the corresponding characteristics of test objects outside. However, for the theoretical interpretation which we give to these facts it *is* essential that similar effects be demonstrated outside a given percept. It is here that the *field* of a percept should extend, if interaction between percepts is due to the existence of such a field; and the current-theory of the field clearly demands that prolonged inspection lead to after-effects outside the percept just as it does within its area. Between the two cases there should be a difference merely of degree. Such a quantitative difference would follow from the fact that the current outside can spread more widely, and will thus be less densely distributed than the inner current.

The fifth experiment answers the question which

93

has just been raised. Both test objects now lie outside the area which during the inspection period is surrounded by the figure outline, for instance, an oblong (*cf*. fig. 10). If the left test object is at all influenced it should, because of its distance from the figure, at least be less altered than the right one. The observation confirms this expectation: the right square is much smaller, and it lies back in space.—In this example the right test object is still in contact with the figure. This is by no means necessary. Experiments

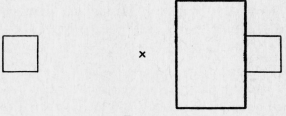

FIG. 10

like the present can be repeated when the nearer test object lies outside the figure area and several millimeters removed from the next contour. The effect is still obvious so long as the other test object remains much farther distant from the figure area. Thus it is shown that a figure is functionally active in its homogeneous environment, and that in this sense a percept is surrounded by a field whose intensity decreases as the distance increases.

6. We have no difficulty in demonstrating *three* degrees of the after-effect in one perceptual situation.

In the following pattern (fig. 11), one test object lies inside the figure area, a second one just outside, and a third much farther away. After prolonged inspection (10 minutes[1]) the lowest square appears much smaller

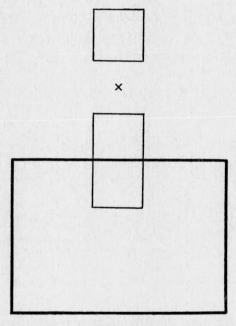

Fig. 11

than its neighbor just outside, and the distant square is larger than the two others. The straight vertical contour of these is again "broken" in the way which has been described in experiment 4.

[1] Much less than this will suffice in most cases. In our first experiments we tended to choose unnecessarily long inspection periods.

7. One might be inclined to believe that these effects are all due to some unknown influence which a *contour* as such has upon its immediate neighborhood. This can only mean that the effect in a given region will be the stronger, the more contour there is in the neighborhood of this region. As a matter of fact, if this may be called an explanation, it surely fits all observations which have as yet been described. The next experiment, however, is specially arranged as a test of this view (fig. 12). The edges of the

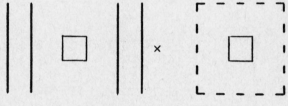

FIG. 12

square on the right side are actually *broken* lines; the interruptions of these lines amount to 3/5 of their total length. The four parallel lines on the left side, which have the same length as the edge of the square, are continuous; the distance of the inner pair has again the same length. One can easily convince oneself that the test object on the right side is surrounded by *less* contour than limits the open area on the left in which the second test object is situated.[1]

[1] The contours of the test objects are actually not thinner than are those of the inspection pattern.

If we consider merely the inner pair of the continuous lines on the left side we find that their total length is about 25% greater than that of the four broken contours of the figure on the right; and distances of the contours from the test objects are in this pattern directly comparable. From this point of view we must therefore expect the stronger effect, if any, to be found on the left side. Actually, after the inspection period (say, 6 minutes) the test object on the left side is found to be undoubtedly larger (and, for the author, nearer) than the test object on the other side.

This agrees with the current-theory. For fairly obvious reasons the current inside the figure on the right side cannot leave this figure in spite of its broken edges, and thus it must remain concentrated in this area. On the other hand, there is no reason why the current which pervades the corresponding area on the left side should not spread beyond this area both above and below, and thus become less dense.

8. The procedure which has been used in these experiments is not entirely satisfactory. It is cumbersome to fixate a point for several minutes in preparation for an observation which takes no more than a few seconds. To be sure, the persistency of the after-effect makes it possible to test several regions in and around a given figure in quick succession, when this figure has once been inspected for a number of minutes. It would, however, be much more convenient if the after-effect, and thus the current-distribution

for a given pattern, could be made visible for all regions of the field at the same time. The way in which the distribution of a magnetic field is demonstrated with the help of iron-filings appears as an ideal which one would gladly imitate in the present case. Several attempts have been made in this direction. We prepared test screens which contained regular distributions of small figures or other simple but extensive patterns, and hoped that differential effects as to local size, depth, and brightness would demonstrate in a simultaneous view how the parts of such patterns are influenced by previous inspection of a figure. But we have not yet found a pattern that gives any clear effects. It seems that the very regularity of such designs counteracts any differences in the appearance of their parts which the previous inspection would otherwise produce. This appears the more likely since one has merely to remove most of the extensive design in order to make the field effect quite striking for the remaining parts. It is to be hoped that in a further investigation of these problems some such simple demonstration of the field distribution as a whole will still be discovered. For the time being the slower procedure remains necessary.

9. Clumsy though this technique may appear, it can undoubtedly be used for an unlimited number of further observations. I will indicate merely one more direction of inquiry. Test objects show a considerable change in size when they are located within

a region which has been strongly influenced by a figure. This means that the after-effects of figure processes tend to *distort* given visual objects. In our previous experiments, however, few distortions in a more specific sense, i.e., alterations of *shape,* have been demonstrated. We have to expect such altera-

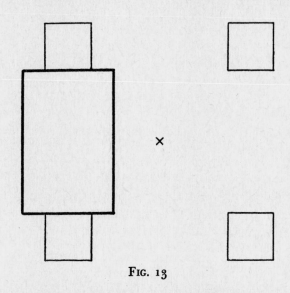

FIG. 13

tions under conditions in which the test objects constitute a specific pattern, which lies partly in a strongly altered region, and partly in a zone in which merely weak after-effects, if any, have been produced. This is the case in the next experiment (fig. 13). The test objects on the left do not merely have a size in themselves. These objects may also be considered as the ends of a vertical distance, and this distance falls entirely into the area of the previously inspected figure. It should therefore appear as shortened just as the test objects will be too small, because they lie in a region in which the outside current has great density. The test objects on the right, and the distance between them, are probably so far apart from the figure that no comparable effect can be expected in their case. As a consequence the symmetrical pattern of the test objects should be distorted. It should not remain a square; rather it should appear as a trapezoid whose shorter parallel edge is the distance on the left.

In the present form this experiment is not the most striking demonstration of the principle with which out investigation is concerned. The test objects, it is true, appear as a trapezoid. At the same time the squares on the left side are of course smaller than are those on the right side; their edges are paler, and for most observers these squares lie farther back in space. But the effect is much more conspicuous if, in a simple variation of the experiment, the vertical distance between the test objects is reduced so that those on the left side fall inside the area of the oblong.

Incidentally, for several observers the shortening of the vertical distance on the left side shows a curious asymmetry. The lower test object is more strongly displaced in the upward direction than is the upper test object in the downward direction. The problems with which we are here occupied seem at this point to merge with those which concern the "anisotropy" of visual space (*cf.* ch. I, pp. 15 ff.)

10. At about this stage of our observations it occurred to us that a recent discovery of Gibson's must be a special case of the same after-effects.[1] Gibson found that, when a subject inspects a slightly curved line for a number of minutes, the curvature of this line tends to decrease, and that after the inspection period a perfectly straight line appears as curved in the opposite direction. An analogous effect was observed in the case of a bent line, i.e., of two straight lines which meet at a large obtuse angle. The angle between the lines seemed to approach 180°, and thus the bent line to approximate the straight form. After the inspection period a straight line appeared bent in the opposite direction. The mere fact that these effects were observed as a result of prolonged inspection points to a common cause of our own and Gibson's observations. This interpretation acquires a high degree of probability in view of the fact that in the last experiment we have also been able to demonstrate an actual distortion of the test pattern.

There is merely one point at which Gibson's work seems at first to be at odds with the scheme in which we see our own observations. He wanted to decide whether his effect was *localized,* or whether it affected

[1] J. Gibson, Journ. of Exper. Psychol. *16* (1933).

appropriate test objects everywhere in the field. His tests decided in favor of the first assumption. However, before we argue that in this respect Gibson's discovery differs from our own experiments we should define what we mean by a localized effect. In a sense our experiments, too, demonstrate localized after-effects. Test objects appear as changed within, and in the neighborhood of, figures; and the very principle of our observations implies that these changes are far less conspicuous if test objects lie at a greater distance from the area of the previously inspected figure. On the other hand, Gibson's own statements make it quite clear that he does not use the term localization in an absolute sense. In fact, since his inspection objects and his test lines can have no more than two points in common, it is for geometrical reasons almost impossible to contend that his effect is local in that strict sense. If, as is the case in Gibson's experiments, merely a line is inspected, the alteration of the medium may not extend quite so far as it does in our observations. But, if we assume that as a matter of principle his discovery must be classed with our own experiments, at least some extension of his effect beyond the location of the inspection object must be demonstrable. For this purpose the following pattern can be used (fig. 14). We draw two parallel curves at a distance, say, of 3 cms. and have the subject fixate a point between them. After the inspection period we remove the curves and show a straight line (with a fixation point at the middle), which at no point touches the places in which the curves appeared beforehand. This straight line is now seen as curved in the opposite direction. For obvious reasons its curved shape is more conspicuous near its ends than in the

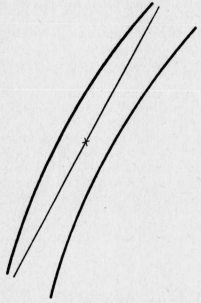

FIG. 14

middle. On this further evidence we are surely justified in regarding the Gibson effect as a particular case within the same group of facts as have been described in the last pages. Thus this effect must also find a place in the wider theoretical scheme which led to our experiments. We shall, however, not yet try to explain why in this case prolonged inspection leads to changes of curvature and of direction. Any such attempt will be premature until simpler forms of the after-effect have been more fully understood.

It seems advisable to mention a few points which should be kept in mind when any of these experiments are repeated. I remarked already that a given after-effect will easily interfere with new ones if experiments are not sufficiently spaced in time. It is equally essential that test patterns be checked as to their appearance when no inspection period has preceded; because in certain retinal positions objects will under all circumstances be slightly distorted or reduced in size. Again, both during the inspection period and the test the subject should carefully avoid any major movements of the eyes and the head. As soon, for instance, as he bends his head to one side, a test object may no longer lie within the region which the test is meant to explore. And one can easily show that in this case the appearance of the test pattern may change entirely. It should also be remembered that the test objects themselves are figures which must tend to exert a similar influence upon the field. Observation of these objects should therefore be restricted to a few seconds. Nor does this constitute a difficulty: any after-effects which are not at once visible will generally allow of diverse interpretations.

The changes which test patterns undergo in these experiments have not yet been *measured*.[1] In fact, this has not seemed to be our most urgent task, since everybody can easily convince himself of the facts as such. On the other hand, we have no doubt as to the

---

[1] The Gibson effect has of course been measured.

possibility of measuring the more striking effects. In experiment 9, for instance, the distance between the test objects on one side of the trapezoid is so much shortened that we should have no difficulty in compensating for this change by a corresponding variation of the distance between the test objects on the other side. Some such technique will be used as soon as our problems and our theory are far enough developed for making quantitative experiments more useful than they would have been during our first exploratory observations. And it goes without saying that no more than a preliminary survey has here been given.

In any case it should be emphasized that in these experiments our primary interest is not concentrated on the after-effects as such. They are facts which probably have no great importance in ordinary vision; we do not as a rule fixate a given point for any length of time. The first and main import of these observations lies in their significance for the general theory of percepts and of percept fields. From this point of view the after-effects of prolonged inspection assume value to the extent to which they indicate that a percept field spreads in and around a figure. For there cannot be any after-effect in places in which nothing has happened by which it could be produced. And the varying degree which the after-effect attains in one place or another bears witness to the varying intensity of the process by which it has been caused. Thus our principal assumption, the current-theory of percepts, can be tested.

Sooner or later, it is true, the theory of percept fields will have to be completed by an equally definite theory of their after-effects as such. Then this theory, too, will contribute to our understanding of perception in general. Strong after-effects distort the visual field. Once we learn just what changes in the medium lead to such distortions, we shall also have new evidence as to the relation between perceptual facts and their somatic correlates.

CHAPTER III

RETENTION AND RECALL

I

THE VALUE of biological theories in psychology is not generally recognized. There are, for instance, those who believe that any such attempts must lead to a misrepresentation of mental life. I have elsewhere tried to explain why I cannot share this distrust.[1] Moreover, since the intimate connection between mental facts and processes in the nervous system is a matter not of speculation but of observation, it would seem to me an indefensible weakness if we were to close our eyes to the problems which follow from this observation. To be sure, the terms in which the functions of the nervous system are generally discussed cannot appeal to anybody who is aware of the principal characteristics of mental activities. To a considerable extent these activities are felt to be "sensible" with regard to the situations to which they refer; or, more cautiously speaking, with regard to these situations *as we see them*. The usual interpretation of neurological facts, on the other hand, gives us no analogue to any such reasonable relationship

[1] W. Köhler, *The Place of Value in a World of Facts* (1938), ch. 6 and ch. 10.

between situations and mental activities. According to these theories a "response" follows a "stimulus" because an indifferent neural "connection" between one and the other has been sufficiently reinforced in previous life. Just the opposite "response" would follow the same "stimulus," and would do it with the same ease, if reinforcements had sufficiently strengthened this opposite "connection." Thus, while our experience says that we can act reasonably, the neurological theory implies that this is sheer mysticism; that actually situations and human actions are no more sensibly connected than is the cargo of one freight car and that of the next.

In the last analysis human civilization seems to be based on the conviction that ultimately certain things are intrinsically sensible and ought to be pursued, whereas others are against sense and must be prevented. I sympathize with those who share this conviction, and I dislike doctrines which ignore obvious experiences and also threaten to destroy the very fundament of human culture. But I cannot admit that this danger becomes any less imminent if we turn our eyes away from the field of psychophysical relations in which these doctrines have arisen. Our reaction should not be: Let us have a psychology which ignores neurology. This in itself would be unreasonable in view of the intimate relations between mental and biological facts. It would thus constitute a denial of just the principle which we wish to defend. The only policy which is in line with this principle consists in a serious effort to give the psychophysical problem a solution which deserves this name. After all, we need not worry. The neurological speculations to which we object consist in an entirely unwarranted application of certain data about primitive nerve function and primitive automatisms to those activities of the brain which are associated with essential mental processes. Any adequate attempts to construct the correlates of these processes will have to use as their primary evidence the characteristics of such mental facts. For this purpose we shall have to analyze the functional meaning of the terms "sensible" and "reasonable"; and no brain activity will satisfy us as a correlate of reasonableness which does not exhibit the same functional characteristics. The general point of view which underlies this procedure is called *isomorphism*. It can be derived from the principle of evolution.[1] Its content is that the structural properties of experiences are at the same time the structural properties of their biological correlates. The principle of isomorphism seems to hold in some parts of psychology. If it should apply to mental life as a whole, the psychophysical problem would lose its threatening character entirely.

We understand the motives of those who fear that neurological theories of mental life will always try to explain reasonableness in terms of senseless mecha-

[1] W. Köhler, *loc. cit.*, pp. 390-396.

nisms. But why should psychologists, who have no such misgivings, show a hostile attitude toward biological theories in their science? And yet, there are some who do so. The world, they say, is distributed among a number of sciences. In psychology we deal with facts of a particular kind. Similarly the physicists, chemists, physiologists, and neurologists are occupied with their special fields. We have just as little reason to interfere in their tasks as they have to meddle with our work.

As an answer I must repeat that mere psychological research gives us a number of rules but no sufficiently coherent framework in which these rules can be combined into a body of systematic knowledge. The threads of purely psychological information disappear everywhere into another domain which is not accessible to our methods. Few psychologists will deny that this other domain is biology. Thus, if we refuse to follow our loose threads into biology, and if we leave it to the biologists to see where such threads lead, we also leave it to them to transform our sadly incomplete data into an understandable system. In other words, we expect the biologists to give our facts and rules an explanation and a theory. But at its best science has always meant a vivid interplay of observation and theory. "Those who refuse to go beyond fact," said T. H. Huxley once, "rarely get as far as fact." Therefore, if we waited for biology to give us a theoretical framework, we should also have to wait for the biologists to provide us with the best incentives for our factual research.

And we should have to wait a long time. It seems to me irrelevant whether an important advance in science is made by men whom we call psychologists or by others whom we call biologists. But those whom we now call biologists are quite unlikely to solve in the near future just those biological problems which must be approached if psychological research is to obtain a coherent theoretical foundation and corresponding *Fragestellungen*. The biologists show little inclination to attack these tasks, simply because *qua* biologists they have not the data which make precisely such tasks particularly urgent. We, the psychologists, may know little; but we know several things about mental life which we may safely regard as invaluable evidence about the essential functions of the brain. If we combine such evidence with what we know about the physical characteristics of the brain, hypotheses about the correlates of mental facts are likely to emerge from the combination. And hypotheses are tentative theories from which new factual problems will immediately follow. Biologists, on the other hand, are for the most part unconcerned with our psychological evidence. Moreover, like most scientists, they have little confidence in psychological observation. From their point of view an observation must refer directly to the brain if it is meant to count in brain physiology. Are we to work without a theoretical background and without its stimulating influence until biology happens to discover its own approach to the questions in which we are interested? I do not see why we should thus delay the advance of our discipline.

At this point it will be objected that there have been attempts to construct the neurological counterparts of mental life, and that at the present time we still find it difficult to get rid of some erroneous conceptions which were then imported into psychology. Unfortunately, I admit, there have been such errors. But what follows? In chemistry there was once a theory according to which combustion meant the disappearance of phlogiston, in physics a theory which regarded heat as an unweighable material. It will not be argued that for such reasons neither chemistry nor physics should ever have tried a theory again. As a matter of fact, the present objection expresses the emotion of discouragement rather than a scientific argument. It is not good logic to say that, because in one case a particular form of an enterprise has failed, all other enterprises in the same field will also fail. We might quite as well contend that after one abortive attempt to cure tuberculosis we should abstain from any further attempt in this direction; and that, if one League of Nations was a failure, no better construction has any hope of success. Many people who are more strongly influenced by the dynamics of emotional life than by the logic of inferences actually do draw such extraordinary conclusions. But scientists had better refrain from doing the same.

Incidentally, it seems to me, the objection contradicts itself. How do we know that those older neurological theories were wrong? Obviously the argument presupposes that our criticism is well-founded. We know that they were wrong to precisely the extent to which we now know the indispensable prerequisites and factual conditions which those theories did not satisfy; in other words, the conditions which a more adequate theory must henceforth fulfill. With this, however, we have already taken the first step in the development of a better theory.

I hesitate to mention a further objection to biological theory, because it throws a sad reflection upon our scientific courage. Do you really expect us, I have been asked, to study all those branches of science which may be of importance in the theory of brain-function?

Of course nobody can be forced to participate in the solution of a fascinating problem. But is it not depressing that the task of having to travel through several fields of science is sometimes regarded not as an alluring prospect but as a disagreeable demand? What could be more attractive than the study of fields which the human mind has conquered in some of its most magnificent adventures? It is not natural for a human being to be interested merely in one particular phase of experience. If the present situation of psychology offers us an excellent reason—or should I say a marvellous pretext—for extending our curiosity beyond our limited field, should we not rather be impatient to seize this opportunity at once? And let us not believe that in doing so we should dangerously dissipate our energies. Frankly speaking, does it require so much energy to know what is worth knowing in present psychology that no energy is left for more general information in science? Surely the mathematicians and the physicists, whose disciplines are older and correspondingly richer in knowledge, are quite able to cope with much more information than we at present have to carry with us in pure psychology.

On the other hand, it is merely limited amounts of outside information which are likely to be needed in our endeavor. Advance in the physiological knowledge of the nervous system is now much more rapid than it was, say, thirty years ago. None the less, progress in this field can still be easily followed. Actually some psychologists seem to find this task much easier than that of keeping themselves informed in certain branches of psychology; and, I believe, it really is. Thus one cannot say that in this respect the development of biological theories in psychology would overtax our forces. With regard to the sciences of inanimate nature the strain would not be much greater. Our knowledge of the brain as a physical medium is restricted; but even so it shows quite clearly that large divisions of physical science will probably have no application in brain theory. There is no reason why we should study much acoustics, optics, and physics of radiation in general, when we prepare for our task. The fact that all electric phenomena in the brain are of slight intensity tends to exclude electromagnetism and electrodynamics. The thermodynamics of the nervous system is tremendously simplified by the fact that for all initial stages of our work the operations of nervous tissue can be regarded as practically iso-thermic. In fact, the parts of science which we can exclude from our preparations are so numerous and so large that it would be easier to enumerate what we need than what we need not study.[1]

The very best support for our program can be found in the history of science. It would be interesting to inquire how many times essential advances in science have first been made possible by the fact that the boundaries of special disciplines were *not* respected. The greatest progress which astronomy ever made consisted in the discovery that this science has no laws of its own, that astronomy is a part of physics. Later it was found that astronomy is a special field of chemistry, too. Organic chemistry would never have become what it is now, if it had remained separated from common chemistry. Biologists made the

[1] Apart from physical chemistry and electrochemistry, the most important discipline which will have to be included in the list is *potential theory*, the theory of macroscopic self-distributions. Unfortunately this field shares the neglect in which many parts of classical physics have fallen since atomic physics came into the foreground. (*Cf.* W. Köhler, *loc. cit.*, pp. 199-206.)

first important observations on osmotic pressure, which is a purely physical fact. And at the present time it is of course quite customary for physicists to trespass on chemical ground, for mathematicians to do excellent work in physics, and for physicists to develop new mathematical procedures. Everywhere except in psychology it is regarded as an axiom that border regions, in which one discipline is in contact with another, offer the best opportunities for substantial discoveries. Nor is the reason for this fact hard to find. Suppose, for instance, that certain principles actually apply in two fields, but that their relevance is more obvious in one than it is in the other. For those who work in the latter field it will often be highly advisable to look over the boundary into the former. What they see there may help them to realize essential traits of their own facts. More generally, the most fortunate moments in the history of knowledge occur when facts which have been as yet no more than special data are suddenly referred to other apparently distant facts, and thus appear in a new light. For this to happen in psychology we should keep ourselves informed about more than our subject-matter in the narrowest sense. From this point of view it is not the present program which needs to be defended. On the contrary, those who object to it will have to explain why they ignore this impressive lesson of history: trespassing is one of the most successful techniques in science.

But it is biological *theory* which I have recommended. If such a theory were successful it would eventually embrace wide fields of knowledge. It would also embrace them in the sense that some facts in one field would become deducible from facts in other fields. Such an idea seems to be regarded with deep suspicion by some psychologists. Let us have facts, not theories, they would say.

I shall not here repeat Huxley's words. I shall merely say: Important though entirely accidental discoveries may sometimes be, for the most part an experiment about essentials will not occur to anybody unless a good problem leads to it. And a problem arises in a theoretical context. Moreover, just why should we have merely facts, not theories and explanations? In physics, facts and theories form a unitary structure which nobody will be inclined to destroy. Chemistry without any theory is nowadays unthinkable, and so, in a lesser degree, is biology. Why this curious Purism in psychology? It appears that those psychologists who do not like to see their colleagues interested in biology and physics are themselves interested in at least one other discipline besides psychology. This discipline is epistemology. And some psychologists return from short excursions into this field with firmly established creeds which have less to do with things which we ought to do than with others which we should *not* do. Their pronouncements are directed not merely against biological theory in psychology but also against theory in general. We hear that nowadays "explanation is reduced to description," and that "true explanation and observed correlation turn out to be one and the same thing." [1] There seems to be a curious satisfaction in making assertions by which old aspirations of mankind are in no time wiped off the slate of legitimate enterprises. In the present case it used to be held that to a degree there are understandable relations among our experiences, and that to this extent the scientist can go beyond mere descriptions and mere correlations of facts. Apparently we are now invited to regard this as a mere dream.

I do not think that such a denial of any rational content of science can be justified. Take these examples:

One can show as a mere matter of observation that in a state of equilibrium the interior of a charged conductor contains no free electricity, that the charge is located exclusively on the surface. Again, merely observed correlations may lead to the statement that electric charges attract or repel each other according to Coulomb's law. On the other hand, we do not merely state a correlation among our observational data, we do something entirely different, if we deduce Coulomb's law from the fact that the equilibrium distribution of a charge is a surface distribution.

[1] B. F. Skinner, Journ. of General Psychol. 5 (1931); C. C. Pratt, *The Logic of Modern Psychology* (1939), p. 132.

We can make observations on currents, which we summarize as Ohm's law. Other observations may lead us to an empirical rule about the "conservation of electricity." A third set of mere observations which refer to the intensity of currents in branches of a circuit may lead to Kirchhoff's well-known rules. As a scientific activity it is something quite different from the discovery of such factual correlations if we show that, once the first two empirical laws are given, Kirchhoff's rules follow necessarily.[1]

In the same way the electromotive forces between electrolytes of different ionic content *can* be empirically determined. But they can also be deduced from other facts, which principally concern the diffusion of ions. And when we are occupied with this deduction we do something that differs fundamentally from any observation of factual correlations.

I do not wish to enumerate further examples. Physics is to such a degree a system of rational relationships among empirical facts, it contains so much explanation and theory, that a more complete survey would gradually approximate the volume of a textbook of this science. Of course properties of physical systems which can be deduced from other facts should also be directly observed. But if this is done the behavior in question nevertheless remains deducible from those other facts.

[1] So far as I know the deduction of these rules actually preceded their empirical demonstration.

It is hard to believe that such an obvious duality of scientific procedures—first, the observation of facts and of their factual correlations, secondly, the deduction of certain facts from other facts—will be seriously negated by anybody. Those who say that theories are no more than descriptions or statements about factual correlations may be merely using such terms as description and correlation in a new and dangerously wide sense. If I call *any* established connection among facts a correlation, then a connection which I find necessary by deduction will obviously become a "correlation" by virtue of my new use of this term. And the same holds for the word "description." In the meaning of this term I *can* include necessary relationships among facts. But in doing so I am no longer free to say that now I have reduced explanation to description, or that in this way an explanation and an observed correlation become one and the same thing. Certain *names* would become the same in such a misleading terminology, but behind these names the duality of factual information and deductive connection would remain entirely unaffected.

Those who dislike this duality may of course try to demonstrate that in the last analysis deduction is something different from what it seems to be. But at the present time its value as a technique no longer depends upon any such speculations. As a tool in science it is just as indispensable as are observation and measurement. And the critics of theory are surely on the wrong track if they confuse the logical interpretation of this tool with the question whether the tool should be used.

In a recent book Professor C. Pratt argues strongly in favor of biological theories in psychology.[1] But he also shows a tendency to devalue the very procedure which he recommends. Explanations, he says, are necessarily circular. From observed facts we extract their formal characteristics, and then we construct further facts in such a way as to yield precisely the characteristics which are already known.—Is it really quite as simple as that? Pratt uses an astronomical example. When the planet Uranus was found to have an orbit whose shape could not be explained by the Newtonian attraction of the sun and of other known planets, somebody suggested that there might be one more planet beyond Uranus, and that the irregularities in the behavior of Uranus might be due to the influence of this unknown neighbor. This assumption led astronomers to compute the characteristics of a further planet which would give the irregularities in the orbit of Uranus. In doing this, Pratt says, they made use of the same facts as were afterwards explained by the hypothetical further planet. Consequently the procedure was circular; the astronomers projected into this hypothetical planet what they already knew about the strange behavior of Uranus. In this way Professor Pratt prepares his discouraging thesis: "Science is a vast and impressive tautology."

But do we actually say the same things in an explanation as are contained in our observations? Pratt's own example proves that we do not. If I first say: "The orbit of Uranus shows these specific irregularities," and if I then add: "A further (unknown) planet which has a

[1] C. C. Pratt, *The Logic of Modern Psychology* (1939), pp. 129 ff.

certain orbit would give rise to these irregularities of Uranus," I do not merely repeat the content of my former statement in the latter. The statement about Uranus contains not a single word about a further planet.—The same follows from the fact that entirely different hypotheses might be brought forward as explanations of the irregular behavior of Uranus. One might, for instance, boldly assume that Uranus sometimes passes through clouds of dark stellar debris, loses speed during such periods, and consequently exhibits an irregular orbit. Surely, this hypothesis differs widely from that about a further planet. Therefore they cannot both be circular, i.e., tautological, with regard to the same known data about Uranus.

Professor Pratt would answer that in the case of both hypotheses the particular characteristics of the hypothetical agent will have to be computed from the observed behavior of Uranus. This is correct; but on nearer inspection this turns out to be an argument against himself. The hypothesis about an unknown planet leads to certain computations, the explanation by diffuse stellar material to others. Why are the computations different? Simply, because each assumption implies the existence of some factor which exists independently of the irregular behavior of Uranus, and which is a different object in the two cases. Such factors are, however, posited not merely as independent agents; they are also supposed to act according to known laws. In this respect the explanations obviously do not repeat the content of the observations which are to be explained. Rather they refer to general principles concerning either the disturbance of one planet by another or the change of orbit which an attracted object suffers when it loses speed. Neither of these principles is derived from the irregularities of Uranus's orbit. It is true that to the extent to which these principles are here applied to hypothetical agents, the special and quantitative characteristics of these agents cannot be derived from those principles. Such particular characteristics are actually computed from the facts which the astronomer wishes to explain. But even in this computation he has to take account of *two* conditions: not merely of the observations about Uranus, but also of the known principles which the hypothetical factors are assumed to follow in their action. Thus the computation varies with the general nature of the hypothetical agents and with these functional principles.

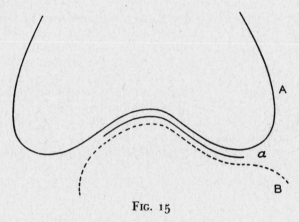

FIG. 15

All this may become clearer if we give it another formulation. A genuine theory of observed facts postulates a structure of further explanatory facts. This structure is defined in terms of known functional properties. It is then maintained that the structure of explanatory facts assumes the form of the observed facts within the region or under the conditions in which the observed facts are actually found. Suppose that the observed facts (say, the irregular behavior of Uranus) can be represented as a curve *a* (*cf.* fig. 15). What we add to *a* in a genuine explanation is not a copy of *a*, but a much wider struc-

123

ture A (say, a new planet which follows Newton's law). This independent structure A, we contend, coincides with a within the limited region of a; but it has no special relation to a outside this region. *A priori* entirely different structures may have this property of coinciding with a within its region—as is indicated in the figure by the further structure B. The principle trait of an actual theory is that the large explanatory structure A (or B) is regarded as indivisible, i.e., that one principle connects all parts of it. From the outset, therefore, this principle must be such as to allow of a as a special case within its domain. And again, consequently, a theory which refers to a can be tested not only in the region a, but at any point within the postulated structure A. This possibility will lead to certain tests for the theory A and to entirely others for the theory B. In the present example, for instance, it has led to the discovery of the new planet Neptune in a predicted position. Professor Pratt does not say how he reconciles this achievement with his belief that explanations are circular.

In many scientific explanations the structure A is *completely* known when the facts a are shown to follow from A as special consequences. Under these circumstances there is not even an appearance of circularity. This is the case, for example, when the electromotive forces between electrolytes of different ionic content are derived from known principles of thermodynamics and diffusion. Here no part of the theory is an "adaption" of A to the particular facts a which the theory explains. The same holds for the current-theory of percepts which has been developed in the second chapter. Among all structures of facts which are known in physics this theory selects one, electrolytical conduction, because electrolytical currents alter the medium through which they pass just as percept processes seem to alter their medium. This particularity of electrolytical conduction is well-known, quite independently of any psychological observations.

Moreover, our knowledge of electrolytical currents is a wide structure; it contains much information to which we did not refer when we first introduced the current-theory. Thus many tests of the theory become possible; because as an indivisible structure of facts the explanatory principle must be adopted as a whole.

II

A set of observed data can be compared with a curve in space. The content of a theory, on the other hand, is like a wide structure of further facts and functional principles which assumes the particular form of the observed data within the region in which such data actually occur. This opens the way to certain examinations of a theory. For inasmuch as the theory is an extensive scheme it must imply consequences beyond the "region of data" which it was originally meant to explain; and these consequences can be tested.

There is, however, a second way in which the scope of a theory tends to grow beyond the region of its original application. If the first procedure examines what new facts may follow from the theory, the second asks whether, conversely, further available data must not be interpreted in terms of the same theory. This will happen when the explanation is first used in one special field, and if it is then found that data in another field are strikingly akin to those in the first. In psychology, for instance, we may try to develop a theory which refers to the retention of nonsense syllables. But obviously retention is not one thing in the case of nonsense syllables and a wholly different thing in the case of other materials. Thus, we shall have to give the theory a much wider application if it is to be accepted in any particular region.

I have—in chapter II—described a few instances of the first procedure as it can be used in connection with the current-theory of percepts. We shall now consider to what extent other available facts demand a similar interpretation. In this respect it will be wise to distinguish clearly between the characteristics of a field theory in general and the particular form which such an explanatory scheme assumes when it is specialized into a current-theory. We shall begin with a discussion in terms of the more general principle.

A psychological fact which seems to allow of no other interpretation than the field principle is *recall*. About fifty years ago Höffding argued that no association in the usual sense of the word could lead to any corresponding recall unless the way were prepared for this event by a selective effect of similarity. Suppose, he said, that two mental contents c and d are associated with each other. If later on a new mental fact C occurs, which has exactly the same properties as c, this new fact is nevertheless not c itself. More particularly, C is not associated with d, although c is. If, therefore, the appearance of C leads to the recall of d, this can happen only because C becomes first of all functionally related to c, or rather to the memory trace of c. Once this has happened, we shall probably find a way in which the transition from c to d, and thus the recall of d, can be understood. Without a connection $C-c$, on the other hand, recall of d upon the appearance of C would remain a miracle. Now, what condition can make for a functional relation between C and c rather than between C and any other memory traces? Surely, C and c are not "associated," because this individual event C occurs now for the first time. Consequently, Höffding said, the connection $C-c$ cannot result from any previous experience; it must be due to a direct effect of their similarity. In this sense any recall on the basis of a previous "association" presupposes, if we follow Höffding, a more immediate process, the selection of c by C, for which there is no other reason than their kinship.[1]

Höffding's argument was gradually forgotten under the influence of certain neurological ideas. According to these notions an association is formed when a process c and a process d arrive in the brain, each on its particular nerve path, but at about the same time and not too far distant from each other. It is assumed that under these circumstances a specific bond between the locus of c and that of d is established or strengthened. If afterwards "the process c occurs again" it will travel along the c-path and, since it here finds a particular bond that leads to the locus

[1] H. Höffding, *Psychologie* (1887), p. 196.

of the trace d, it will proceed in this direction, and bring d back to life. In this scheme it is silently taken for granted that all processes which have the characteristics of c must take the same route, the c-path. Evidently, if this be accepted, Höffding's argument loses all force; the fact that all representatives of the class c prefer to keep on one track makes it unnecessary to introduce any selective effect of similarity. All members of this class will arrive at one locus in the brain; and, once they are in this place, the bond of association will take care of their delivery at the locus of d.[1]

That this scheme does not work was first shown by the physiologist von Kries, who thereby gave new power to Höffding's argument.[2] According to von Kries, processes of given properties are by no means restricted to one route in the nervous system. The same figure can be seen in foveal vision, or it can be projected upon various more peripheral parts of the retina. Under these circumstances the process which corresponds to the figure will travel on correspondingly different tracks, and it will arrive at different parts of the visual center of the brain. If we now show an unknown figure in one retinal position, will this figure be recognized when later on it is shown in another position? Again, if in its first

[1] *Cf.* W. Köhler, *Gestalt Psychology* (1929), p. 343 f.
[2] J. von Kries, *Ueber die materiellen Grundlagen der Bewusstseinserscheinungen* (1901).

place it becomes associated with a word, will this
word be recalled when later the figure is projected on
another part of the retina? As a rule, von Kries said,
it will be; and actually E. Becher showed in special
experiments that von Kries was right.[1] The scheme
which we have just been discussing gives no explanation of this fact. From the new place of the figure
process in the brain many bonds may issue; but there
is no reason why the best among these bonds should
lead from the present place of the figure process to
the place of d. It has sometimes been objected that
all processes, of whatever origin, may leave traces in
a common memory center of the brain, that later
any corresponding processes C may be conducted to
this center, and that they would in this fashion invariably come in contact with their right partners c.
But the scheme cannot be saved by this assumption;
because if C meets the trace c in this center, it also
meets there all other traces which have ever been
deposited in the previous life of the individual. Why,
then, should it select c rather than any other trace for
more intimate intercourse? There is no answer unless
it be Höffding's principle that mere similarity exerts
a selective influence. Thus we are back at the point
at which we started. And once we adopt such an immediate effect of similarity we may as well part with
the notion of a common memory center. It has no
longer any function for our purpose; what it was

[1] E. Becher, *Gehirn und Seele* (1911).

meant to achieve will in any case have to be done by the selective action of similarity.

But for what reason should a process prefer the society of a trace with which it has some or many characteristics in common? Obviously we are now assuming that in *recognition* it is this preference which as a rule makes us recognize things which we actually know, and which makes us regard things as new which are actually not familiar. Again, we are contending with Höffding that all correct recall which is based on an *association* by contiguity occurs solely because the same preference has first made a process C select a kindred trace c. Moreover, if similarity has such immediate effects as to the functional relations between C and c, why should we deny that mere similarity, apart from any previous association, can lead to *recall by similarity* of c when C is given? In fact, there is much evidence to support this conclusion. It is now neglected merely because we do not know how to explain such an immediate effect of similarity.

I will confess that I have no such explanation myself. On the other hand, the present problem reminds me strongly of a situation with which we have to deal in perception. And, I must say, it would be curious if the functional rôle which similarity plays in recall were not in principle the same as the selective influence which similarity exerts in this other field.[1] So long as no satisfactory explanation can be

[1] *Cf.* above p. 60 ff.

given to either problem it will at least simplify matters if the two problems are shown to be essentially
one problem that assumes slightly different forms in
two different settings. In perception similarity favors
the specific functional relations involved in *grouping*
or in any other formation of perceptual units. We
mentioned this example once before; because it
clearly demands that a theory of perception be a field
theory. Similarity among percepts can have a selective effect as to their functional connection only if
the characteristics of each percept are somehow
represented beyond its locus in a more restricted
sense of this word. Only in this case is there any
reason why a second percept should react differently
to the presence of a first percept, depending upon
whether the properties of this first percept are the
same or entirely different. Our present problem in
memory is functionally identical with this situation
in perception, except for one single point: when
thinking of perceptual patterns we refer for the most
part to configurations which are simultaneously
given. In this case it is a similarity among *processes*
which makes for the formation of specific groups.
The present problem in the field of memory consists
in the fact that a process becomes preferably related
to similar rather than to entirely different *traces*.
However, no sharp dividing line separates these two
situations. The selective influence of similarity on
grouping can be demonstrated just as well in the case

of temporal or successive organization as in the case of simultaneous patterns. It operates in auditory, in visual, and in other perceptual sequences. Under such circumstances perceptual organization is a matter of "young" *traces* no less than of processes. Thus a practically continuous series of instances leads from strictly simultaneous organization in perception through successive organization (which everybody will still regard as a perceptual fact) to the particular situation in memory with which we are now occupied. And at every point in this series the selective effect of similarity remains the same. Now, it would be unreasonable to interpret this effect in one way at the beginning of the series, and to give it a different explanation at the other end. We shall therefore conclude that the selective action, with which recognition and every recall begins, is a field effect in the same sense in which such field effects have been postulated in perception. Nor need we make any new assumptions about the "field" in question. If, for instance, a visual percept C reminds us of a similar fact c, which has occurred in our past, we are no longer free to choose the field of C as we please. This place is occupied by our theory of percept processes according to which C extends by virtue of its *current* beyond the locus of its "nucleus." Or should we attribute *two* fields to C, one which provides for perceptual interaction, and another which takes care of specific relations between C and traces? Nobody will be in-

clined to do such a thing, particularly because both
field-varieties would have precisely the same function, namely, to represent the presence of *C* and its
characteristics beyond its locus in a narrower sense.

It may be asked whether from this point of view
we should also attribute a field to a memory trace.
The answer to this question will depend upon the
assumptions which we make about the nature of the
trace.[1] To a degree, however, our decision in this
respect is again prescribed by our previous steps. We
interpreted grouping in perception as the outcome
of interactions among percept processes; and the only
way of understanding such interactions seemed to us
given in Faraday's view that a single object, in our
case a single percept process, is surrounded by a field.
Now it is perfectly easy to demonstrate that a perceptual group will often be *recognized* not because
its members have specific properties, but because the
group as such has certain characteristics. In this case
the trace of a group reacts to the group-characteristics
of a percept; this reaction occurs on the basis of similarity *as to such group-characteristics.* Consequently
the trace must have these characteristics in common
with a given percept; in other words, the members
of the group-*trace* are still in the same relation of

---

[1] *Cf.* W. Köhler, *loc. cit.,* pp. 239 ff. The most important problem
in this connection refers to the relation between after-effects in the
sense of the second chapter and memory traces. It may be doubted
whether this relation can be as simple as was implied in an earlier
remark of mine. *Cf.,* on the one hand, *loc. cit.,* p. 252, footnote, and,
on the other hand, O. Lauenstein, Psychol. Forsch. 22 (1938).

interaction as prevailed within the group-*percept* before it became a group-trace. For the sake of consistency we must therefore postulate that the members of group-traces are surrounded by fields. And from this point of view it seems quite likely that a group of interacting traces is characterized by a group-field which may slightly extend beyond this group itself. With this premise there is no reason why the same should not hold for individual traces. In the next section we shall come back to this assumption.

To summarize: Whenever in the midst of present mental processes a step is taken back into the past, the specific direction of this step appears to be determined principally by kinship between the processes of the moment and particular traces of the past.[1] This holds for recognition, for recall by similarity as such, and for recall on the basis of an association. The theoretical situation which thus arises closely approximates that concerning specific interaction among percept processes, in which similarity plays exactly the same selective part. The field principle, as it has been introduced into the theory of perception, will therefore have to be applied to the theory of recall in the widest sense of the term. This will be necessary in spite of the fact that in the case of recall interaction occurs between a process and a

---

[1] I hesitate to assert that no other factor besides similarity can have this immediate selective influence. Direct interaction in perceptual processes depends on other factors besides that of similarity. The same may be true in the case of recall.

memory trace. An attempt to apply only the *general* field principle seems, however, almost impossible. At least in those instances in which recognition or recall occurs upon the appearance of a visual percept, the current-theory of the field will have to be extended to the case of recall if we adopt it in the case of perceptual organization.

This particular theory is not yet sufficiently developed for being tested in its extension to such new problems. But the more general view which has been indicated in the last paragraphs does allow of immediate examination. We have practically identified specific interaction in perceptual grouping with specific interaction as a basic event in recognition and recall. As a consequence we must conclude that, beyond the mere influence of similarity, recognition and recall follow the same laws as are known to operate in the formation of perceptual groups.

On nearer inspection it will be found that it is not similarity as such which acts selectively in the formation of perceptual groups. For the most part similarities of various degrees will occur in one perceptual situation; and then specific perceptual units will be formed not simply because their members resemble each other, but because their mutual resemblance is greater than is that of such members and any other parts of the situation. Suppose, for instance, that in an otherwise homogeneous environment only two figures of very similar appearance are simultaneously given. They will tend to be seen as one pair even though the distance between them may be great. If now the situation is complicated by a great many further figures, which are located between and around the first two, their influence on the pair will, generally speaking, be detrimental. *All* figures will tend to form one large group. To this rule there is, however, a notable exception. If the additional figures resemble the members of the pair much less than these resemble each other, the specific pair-unit may be preserved. It will be most likely to survive if at the same time the additional items belong to one class, i.e., if they, too, tend to form a specific unit (*cf.* fig. 16 and fig. 17).

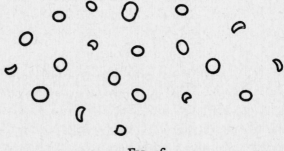

FIG. 16

A slight variation of this example will make its relevance to the problem of recall more obvious. If in fig. 17 only the circle on the left side is first given among the other items, and if then the second circle is added, it will probably form a pair with its partner

on the left. However, if the same is done in fig. 16
the second circle is more likely to become an indifferent member of the group as a whole than to
form a specific unit with the first circle.

This particularity of visual grouping gives us an
opportunity to test the field theory of recall. If specific interaction in recall is essentially the same function as is interaction in perception, the principle of
these examples must be applicable to recall. In other

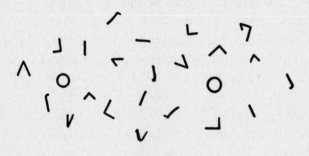

FIG. 17

words, it is not so much similarity as such, as it is
distinctive similarity, which must be the factor that
favors "the step backward" in recognition and in recall. Let us assume that at a certain moment a trace
c is formed, perhaps in association with a trace d.
Experiences of all kinds will follow this event, and
will leave their traces in the nervous system.[1] If now
the percept C appears, which resembles c, it should

[1] As to the representation of past time in the realm of traces
cf. W. Köhler, *loc. cit*., pp. 244 f.

from the present point of view be easily recognized as familiar; or it should remind the subject of *c;* or it should make him remember *d*—provided that the experiences between *c* and *C* (and their traces) do not belong to the same class as *c* (or *C*). What will happen if the opposite is true, i.e., if the experiences between *c* and *C* have much in common with these particular facts? In this case *C* (and probably also the trace of *c*) will tend to become indifferent members of the large and quasi-homogeneous sequence, and the specific "step backward" from *C* to *c* will be less likely to occur. *C* will not easily appear as familiar in any *special* sense; it will not as a rule remind the subject of *c;* and *d* will have little chance of being recalled.

Before we test this inference, however, an essential condition should be realized, which must be fulfilled if the principle of distinctive similarity is to be demonstrated either in perception or in recall. Grouping *can* be influenced by the subject. Once he knows, for instance, that the same two circles are contained in fig. 16 as he has just seen in fig. 17, he will tend to discover the same pair in fig. 16. Under these circumstances the circles will tend to form a specific unit even though *perceptual* conditions do not strongly favor this particular organization. Such a possibility does not contradict the existence of autochthonous principles in perceptual organization; it merely proves that subjective factors may interfere with their operation. We must expect the same to hold for recall. There are two forms of recall: spontaneous recall, which is not expected and not intended by the subject, and intentional recall, in which the subject's "set" is for some reason that of recognizing or recalling. In the latter case the attitude of the subject may strongly interfere with any rules which recall follows without such an influence. More particularly, under these circumstances many a "step backward" may occur which is not solely due to distinctive similarity. Thus, if we wish to show that distinctive similarity influences recall as it does the formation of perceptual pairs, our experiments should test spontaneous rather than intentional recall.

From this point of view Dr. von Restorff, Dr. Bartel, and I designed a number of experiments of which I shall describe a few.[1]

1. A subject is given a series of simple problems. After some have been solved, he is asked to compute x from the equation:

$$21 \ (91/7 + 6) + 14 = x.$$

The subject will begin with the content of the bracket, will find that it is 19, and will now multiply 21 by 19. Unless he is a mathematician he will usually overlook the fact that 21 times 19 equals $(20 + 1) \times (20 - 1)$, and that therefore 21 times 19 amounts to $400 - 1 = 399$. Rather, he will compute the product in the common fashion, which is here less convenient.

[1] *Cf.* W. Köhler and H. von Restorff, Psychol. Forsch. *21* (1935); H. Bartel, Psychol. Forsch. *22* (1937).

When x is found, the experimenter expresses his satisfaction, but he also mentions the more elegant way of multiplying those numbers. This is done in an entirely casual way, as though the remark had no reference to the experiment, and with no hint that any similar task might be given in the future, or that in similar cases the same procedure should be followed. Immediately afterwards further problems are given. One half of the subjects solve other problems of simple arithmetic none of which is, however, likely to remind them of the first task and of the experimenter's remark. The other half are occupied with "match problems" of the familiar kind. In both cases such work is continued for from 10 to 15 minutes, and then, without any interruption or particular information, all subjects are asked to solve as their next task the equation:

$$(15 + 64 - 47)\,28 + (-\ 20 + 34) = x.$$

The first step of the solution leads to the product 32 times 28. This is quite similar to 21 times 19. In the meantime, however, the first group of subjects has been continually occupied with numbers and arithmetical operations, i.e., with experiences of the same general class, whereas the second group has been puzzling about patterns of matches. Subjects in both groups *may* be reminded of 21 times 19 when they are confronted with 32 times 28. But with those of the second group this "interaction backward" should occur more frequently, and the simpler multiplication should be more often used, than is the case with the subjects of the first group. These subjects should be more likely to take the crucial task simply as "the next problem in arithmetic." At least, these expectations follow from the principle of distinctive similarity. The experiment was made with 34 subjects in the unfavorable and with 37 in the favorable constellation, where the terms favorable and unfavorable refer to theoretical expectation. Recall occurred

> in the unfavorable condition 9 times out of 34 cases (26%),
> in the favorable condition 27 times out of 37 cases (73%).

Each individual problem was solved on a special sheet of paper.—Lack of any objective evidence of recall during the crucial test did not of course prove that the subject in question had actually never thought of 21 times 19 and of the experimenter's remark. In negative cases we therefore asked the subjects after the completion of their task whether they had not thought of this remark. This again was done in a casual manner. It sometimes happened that upon the subject's answer an apparently negative case had to be counted as positive. However, in all cases without exception, the question was at once understood. All subjects *could* easily remember what had happened; but in the present case the majority had not spontaneously remembered. This shows how necessary it is in the present experiments to test *spontaneous* recall.

This experiment allows of many variations. Dr. von Restorff developed a technique of "description"

in which the subjects describe or interpret meaningless objects, which are successively shown, and also
indicate whatever ideas may occur to them during
the description. Otherwise the procedure provides
again for two different occupations which follow after
a first event c (the description of a particular class
of objects) and precede a similar event C (the description of an object that greatly resembles c). In
the favorable case objects of another class are interpreted during this period; in the unfavorable situation objects are described which belong to the same
general type as c and C. The problem is whether
during the description of C its partner c is more often
mentioned when the situation is theoretically favorable. 20 subjects were tested in both constella-
tions. Recall occurred

> in the unfavorable condition 3 times out of 20
> cases (15%),
> in the favorable condition 15 times out of 20
> cases (75%).

With a slightly different procedure the corresponding
figures were

> in the unfavorable condition 7 times out of 20
> cases (35%),
> in the favorable condition 16 times out of 20
> cases (80%).

Dr. Bartel invented a third procedure in which the
subjects solve a number of simple technical prob-

lems. During one of the first tasks (c) their attention is casually called to an instrument which in this case may be used as a help. Afterwards one half of the subjects are given problems of the same general type, for which, however, the instrument is of no use; the other half is occupied with tasks of an entirely different class. Without any interruption both groups receive now a problem C which strongly resembles c, and which will be most easily solved if the instrument is once more used. Will this be done more often in one constellation than it is in the other? Recall in this sense occurred

in the unfavorable condition 5 times out of 22 cases (23%),

in the favorable condition 18 times out of 22 cases (82%).

When the experiment was repeated with other subjects results were positive

in the unfavorable condition 2 times out of 12 cases (17%),

in the favorable condition 11 times out of 12 cases (92%).

The probability is undoubtedly small that such great differences result from mere chance five times in succession. Moreover, if the *number* of similar interpolated tasks is varied, the frequency of recall varies in a way which corresponds with theoretical expectations.[1] It seems to follow that principles of perceptual organization are at the same time principles of recall. Thus we have good reasons to extend the field theory to the problem of recall.

III

The experimental procedure which has just been described is in an essential respect identical with the technique by which retroactive inhibition is shown to grow stronger if the inhibiting processes resemble the inhibited material.[2] One might therefore feel inclined to believe that our experiments about the influence of distinctive similarity on recall are simply experiments on retroactive inhibition, and that for this reason the interpretation of the results in terms of field theory becomes superfluous.

I admit that between retroactive inhibition and the facts which have been discussed in the last section there must be some theoretical relation. But this relation cannot be so direct as to make the present experiments mere repetitions of investigations on retroactive inhibition. In the first place, there is a major difference as to the psychological conditions which prevail in our experiments and those on retroactive inhibition. When retroactive inhibition is investigated the subjects are asked to recall to their best ability; the instruction directs their attention to a

[1] *Cf.* H. Bartel, *loc. cit.*
[2] *Cf.* ch. I, p. 32 f.

particular period of the past, and they try to resusci-
tate from this prescribed period whatever they can.
In our experiments no such instruction is given. At
the crucial moment the subjects are occupied with
present activities, and the experimenter takes great
care to avoid any reference to previous parts of the
experiment. If recall occurs, it is as spontaneous and
objectively determined as it can possibly be made.
This is by no means a minor point. If our subjects
had been asked about c when C was given they would
have always recalled c, although in the unfavorable
condition many were not spontaneously reminded of
c. In other words, if the procedure which is usual in
experiments on retroactive inhibition had been applied, no retroactive inhibition whatsoever would
have been discovered.[1] In fact, if any subjects had
been found to be entirely oblivious of c in these simple situations, we should have suspected them of
being pathological cases.

There is a second fact which makes it inadvisable
to interpret such results in terms of retroactive inhibition. Bartel examined cases in which merely *one*
task between c and C belonged to the same general
class as c and C themselves. Even under these circumstances spontaneous recall was clearly less fre-
quent than it was when no such similar event oc-

---

[1] In all negative cases, I repeat, the subjects' attention was cautiously called to the previous event c. They were then found to
know just as much about it as did the other subjects.

curred between c and C.[1] Experiments on retroactive inhibition show no comparable sensitivity of recall to interpolation of related materials.

Moreover, what is retroactive inhibition itself? If we were to subsume the present experiments under this category we should not say much more than that in both cases the interpolation of similar events is detrimental to recall. In fact, we are just as much in need of an analysis of retroactive inhibition as of further exploration of spontaneous recall. And it will soon become apparent that retroactive inhibition itself must be a field effect.

Bartel's experiments on spontaneous recall show clearly that similar events which follow c and precede C may impede recall either by their influence upon c, or upon C, or upon both c and C. It is impossible to interpret his results as though interpolation of kindred material made only c less reproducible. On the contrary, often it is undoubtedly C which combines with preceding similar events, and is thus no longer available for specific interaction with c. As a first step in the analysis of retroactive inhibition we shall now raise the same problem with regard to this effect. Is retroactive inhibition precisely what the name indicates, a detrimental influence of later events upon the products of previous learning? Actually it might also be in part a disturbance of *recall*.

Experiments which were made by Dr. I. Müller

[1] H. Bartel, *loc. cit.*, experiments 6, 8, 10, 11, 12.

throw some light upon this problem.[1] Her subjects memorized (in two presentations) a short main series which contained, besides 2 pairs of syllables and 5 pairs of two-place numbers, 2 pairs of meaningless figures. After 27 minutes all subjects were tested by the method of paired associates. But there were four groups of subjects who were differently occupied during this period. A first group had to learn immediately 4 further short series; a second group did the same 10 minutes after the learning of the main series; a third group did the same 22 minutes after the first learning, i.e., immediately before the test; and the fourth or control group learned no such interpolated series at all. In each group the time not occupied by interpolated learning was filled with the solution of intelligence tests. The 4 interpolated series each contained 6 meaningless figures and 3 two-place numbers. Retention of *these* series was tested directly after their presentation. The experiment was planned mainly to test the influence which the interpolated *figures* had on the retention of the figures in the main series. For this reason I extract from Dr. Müller's tables those data which refer to the reproduction of these figures. The following table contains the results of three such experiments. The words "beginning," "middle," and "end" indicate at what time in the interval the interpolated series were given. From the number of cases which is mentioned

[1] I. Müller, Psychol. Forsch. 22 (1937).

for each result the number of subjects can immediately be seen; it is half the number of the cases. Results are given in terms of correct reproductions.

TABLE III

Control	Beginning	Middle	End
23 out of 30 77%	11 out of 32 34%	6 out of 32 19%	1 out of 32 3%
28 out of 36 78%	13 out of 34 38%	7 out of 32 22%	4 out of 36 11%
18 out of 26 69%	16 out of 26 62%	11 out of 26 42%	9 out of 26 35%

In the third of these experiments the figures of the main series were different from those in the two other series; they were much easier to learn and to retain.

The same procedure was used in a fourth experiment except that the main series now contained 2 single figures, 2 single syllables, and 5 numbers, that the control group was regarded as superfluous, and that the main series was tested by the method of free recall. Results were

Beginning	Middle	End
25 out of 36 69%	23 out of 38 61%	9 out of 36 25%

When the figures were replaced by syllables in the interpolated series, results were not clear so long as the method of paired associates was used; but they showed exactly the same trend when free recall was tested.

It is obvious in these experiments that recall was greatly disturbed as the interpolated activity approached the test in time. It was afterwards discovered that years ago Whiteley had found a disturbance of recall which was caused by interpolated activities given immediately before the test.[1] A similar tendency can be noticed in some of Professor McGeoch's experiments.[2] Thus it might appear for a moment as though retroactive inhibition were not really a retroactive effect; as though this disturbance would have to be referred to the test and the process of recall rather than to the products of previous learning. There are, however, several facts which speak strongly against this radical change of interpretation. I shall not discuss these facts. I will merely mention that in recent experiments at Swarthmore, in which the total interval between learning and test was very long and constant, recall tended to improve when interpolated activities were removed from the immediate neighborhood of learning; but that recall deteriorated again when those activities approached the time of the test.[3] The most plausible view of the theoretical situation may therefore be represented by the following curve (fig. 18). The disturbance or loss is very great when the interpolated material follows the learning directly; it gradually decreases when the interpolated series follow learning after some interval; but it once more becomes stronger when

---

[1] P. L. Whiteley, Journ. of Exper. Psychol. *10* (1927).
[2] J. A. McGeoch, Journ. of General Psychol. *9* (1933).
[3] These experiments were conducted by Professor E. Newman. They are not yet completed.

these series are given immediately before the test. In I. Müller's experiments this situation cannot become apparent because the total interval between learning and test is too short. This prevents the two regions of greater disturbance from separating; the second of these regions is superimposed upon the very beginning of the first; and as a consequence

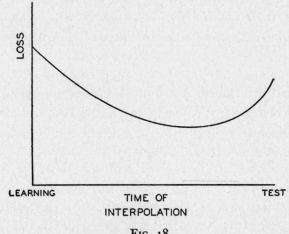

FIG. 18

the disturbance steadily increases as the interpolated activities approach the test in time.

But why is the loss particularly great when these activities are given shortly before recall? I. Müller discusses two possibilities. One can assume that, quite apart from retroactive inhibition, the interpolation of similar material impedes the process of recall. The traces of this material might act like a screen between the product of learning and the present; and the screen might be the less permeable the younger the traces of which it consists. In this case the disturbance of recall would indeed become stronger as the disturbing material approaches the test in time. As a second possibility one might contend that retroactive inhibition in the usual sense is a partly *reversible* effect, that its influence upon the product of learning is strong when the traces of the interpolated material are young, but that the influence decreases when these traces grow older. From this point of view retroactive inhibition as such would be very intense when the interpolated material follows soon after learning; but this initial effect would gradually be lessened if sufficient time elapses before the test. On the other hand, retroactive inhibition as such would tend to be weaker when the interpolated material follows late after learning; but less time would now be available before the test, in which the inhibitory effect could partially subside. Thus the disturbance would remain particularly effective.

Both assumptions seem to agree with the facts which are known at the present time. In one respect they even agree with each other: Both contain the hypothesis that the disturbing effect of interpolated traces is a function of their age; more concretely, that during their youth these traces exert a stronger disturbing influence than they do later, when they are older. The two assumptions differ in that one assumes besides retroactive inhibition a special disturbance of recall, whereas the other assumes only a disturbance of the products of learning, i.e., retroactive inhibition in the usual sense.

The latter hypothesis is simpler. But it also has a second advantage. Disturbances which are strictly analogous to retroactive inhibition occur within a given product of learning itself.[1] It would not be an easy task to interpret these effects as disturbances only of recall; it seems much more plausible to assume that they are located within the product of learning as such. If this is the case, retroactive inhibition, which is so obviously a mere variation of the same effects, must also be a disturbance of the product of learning. Moreover, from this point of view one more fact in the field of memory falls at once in line with those which we are here discussing. This fact is *reminiscence*. Recall is quite often appreciably better when more time has elapsed after learning than it is at an earlier period. This phenomenon obviously corresponds to the observation that in the case of retroactive inhibition recall improves if some time elapses between the interpolated activities and the test. We have explained this observation by assuming that retroactive inhibition is to some extent reversible, i.e., that the traces of interpolated activities are less effective as a disturbance when they have reached a certain age. Thus from the present assumption

[1] *Cf.* ch. I, p. 35 f.

that retroactive inhibition and inhibition within a product of learning are basically the same disturbance, we are immediately led to the conclusion: reminiscence, too, is due to the fact that disturbing effects of traces upon other traces tend to subside in the course of time. In this step no new hypothesis is involved. It is merely consistent to say that inhibition within a product of learning is partly reversible just as is retroactive inhibition.

In a tentative way the reversible nature of these inhibitions may be explained as follows: Percept processes are surrounded by currents. To the extent to which traces have properties in common with their parent-processes, they will also be surrounded by a halo of current.[1] Traces, however, can be regarded as a sediment in the nervous system which must be exceedingly "crowded" within the dimension of past time. As a consequence any field effects among these traces will be very strong; and individual traces will often not be identifiable because they lie to such a degree within the field of their neighbors. There are, however, good reasons for assuming that this situation does not remain the same forever. As time goes on the intensity of those currents is likely to decrease. If this happens, a given trace will gradually emerge from the cloud of current which has temporarily made it inaccessible; and consequently a specific function of this trace as an individual will again be-

[1] W. Köhler, *loc. cit.*, p. 243 f.

come possible. Thus we can understand the fact that both retroactive inhibition and inhibition within a product of learning are partly reversible.

We may now return to the experiments on recall which were described in the second section. Their relation to retroactive inhibition was very much in need of elucidation. This relation will become clearer if we take account of the fact that both retroactive inhibition and inhibition within a product of learning presuppose an accumulation of much disturbing material. In the experiments in which only *spontaneous* recall was impeded, no comparable accumulation occurred. Moreover, individual events and their traces were here more specifically characterized than are syllables or figures in all experiments on retroactive inhibition. It follows that in experiments on retroactive inhibition (and on inhibition within a given learning product) a much more crowded condition of traces is established, and that at the same time these traces are less individually characterized than is the case when only spontaneous recall is made difficult. Now we know that in perception the field-influences among percepts may assume such an intensity as to give rise to actual distortions and to "camouflage." Under these circumstances a given percept may simply disappear, inasmuch as it is absorbed into a larger organization.[1] No such extreme effects will be

[1] W. Köhler, *Gestalt Psychology* (1929), pp. 198-212.

observed in looser groups such as that, say, of fig. 16. Here, it is true, the formation of a particular pair is impeded by the influence of the larger aggregate; but we can easily identify the individual members of this aggregate; and, if we *search* for a particular member we shall soon find it.

The difference between retroactive inhibition and a disturbance solely of spontaneous recall is, I believe, strictly comparable to this difference between two situations in perception. In the case of retroactive inhibition (and its analogue within a given product of learning) traces are so poorly characterized, and at the same time so densely "crowded," that an individual trace can no longer function according to its intrinsic nature. It is too strongly embedded within the field of its neighbors. On the other hand, the experiments which demonstrate a disturbance of spontaneous recall refer to traces whose condition is comparable to that of individual members in the aggregate of fig. 16. When a search is made, i.e., when recall is *intended,* such traces will function quite properly. But in the absence of this additional factor, when only distinctive similarity between present processes and such traces can lead to specific interaction, recall will become infrequent, just as spontaneous formation of a specific pair is improbable in the perceptual analogue. To this first difference between retroactive inhibition and the disturbance of spontaneous recall we must of course add a second. It consists in the fact that a disturbance of spontaneous recall is often due to interaction between a present *process* and traces which have just been interpolated.

It will be observed that the present application of the field principle to questions of memory leads to a strongly unitary theory. Superficially, recall appears as an event which has little in common with factors by which retention and recall are *disturbed*. And yet the present theory assumes that it is essentially the same basic principle which is responsible both for recall and for those disturbances. Recall is here interpreted as an interaction which presupposes a field relation between a particular process and a particular trace. But retroactive inhibition, the inhibition within one product of learning, and the disturbance of spontaneous recall are all attributed to the fact that other traces, too, have their fields which extend in the same medium. Thus the field action between a process and a particular trace, which is implied in recall, may be obstructed by field action for which those other traces are responsible.

INDEX

von Restorff, H., 34 f., 139, 141
Robinson, E. S., 33
Rosenblueth, A., 75
Rubin, E., 22 f., 68

von Schiller, P., 60
Scholz, W., 57 f.
Skinner, B. F., 118
Spiegel, H. G., 58 f.

Stern, W., 16
Stratton, G. M., 24, 28

Werner, H., 59
Wertheimer, M., 44, 59 ff., 67
Whiteley, P. L., 33, 149

Zeigarnik, B., 44